SOCIAL THEORY

WILLIAM OUTHWAITE

P

PROFILE BOOKS

First published in Great Britain in 2015 by
PROFILE BOOKS LTD
3 Holford Yard
Bevin Way
London WC1X 9HD
www.profilebooks.com

A CIP catalogue record for this book is available from the British Library.

ISBN 978 1 78125 481 3
eISBN 978 1 78283 175 4

Designed by Jade Design www.jadedesign.co.uk

Printed and bound in Italy by L.E.G.O. S.p.A.

The paper this book is printed on is
certified by the © 1996 Forest Stewardship
Council A.C. (FSC). It is ancient-forest
friendly. The printer holds FSC chain of
custody SGS-COC-2061

SOCIAL THEORY

***IDEAS* IN PROFILE**
SMALL INTRODUCTIONS TO BIG TOPICS

CONTENTS

To the memory of Roy Bhaskar (1944–2014),
theorist and comrade

INTRODUCTION

If you are interested in political or economic questions, or culture, or gender or ethnic relations, social theory explains the relations between them. You might like to think of this as 'having it all'.

Take globalisation, which has transformed our world and been a big topic of academic and public discussion since the 1990s. Early accounts stressed the economic aspects and political implications for nation-states, but sociologists quickly pointed out that the globalisation of culture was equally important and, crucially, interrelated with the other dimensions. It's possible to write a perfectly decent book about the globalisation of production, trade or financial markets, but if you're going to focus on the world as a whole, as theories of globalisation aimed to, it makes no sense to chop it up into separate economic, political and cultural domains and treat them in isolation. For one thing, what two social theorists in the middle of the twentieth century called the 'culture industry' is just that: an increasingly global industry employing millions of people. If cultural consumption is about taste, it's also about money and politics ('soft power' or influence). Among the causes of the collapse of communism in Europe at the end of the 1980s was the influence of Western and local rock music, and related movements like punk.

Social theory is the best framework we have for thinking about these relations. Take another term which has been heavily used in the last thirty years, 'modernity'. An economic historian will focus on the rise of markets and wage labour in Europe; a political scientist will focus on the growth of state bureaucracies and political representation in parliaments; a sociologist will talk about the emergence of an 'industrial society' or, in more Marxist language, about 'advanced' or 'late' capitalism. But a broader conception of modernity covering all these dimensions is what we need. Modernity in this sense is future-oriented, focused on the development of new ways of producing goods and organising human social and political relations. This is what social theory has provided over the past few hundred years and particularly since the 1980s.

Social theorists, then, ask the big questions and return to them again and again, in different forms in successive generations. The history of social theory is more like the history of philosophy than a history of science that presents it as a succession of 'discoveries'. But there are parallels with what the twentieth-century historian of science Thomas Kuhn called 'scientific paradigms': exemplary achievements, whether technical or conceptual, such as Lavoisier's discovery of oxygen in 1777, which transformed our understanding of combustion and respiration, and in doing so changed the face of science and human knowledge. Kuhn also used the word 'paradigm' to refer to frameworks of explanation and shared assumptions – what he sometimes called a 'disciplinary matrix'. Paradigms of the first kind tend to lead to those of the second.

We can use the term 'paradigm', as I do in this book, for some classic explanatory attempts in social theory which fed into distinctive styles of social thought and continue to be relevant today. I say attempts, because none of them is accepted without question and most, as we shall see, have been superseded in later decades. But that's not the point; we're interested in them because they introduce *ways* of explaining things. They set theoretical and political agendas. We are still, for example, thinking about inequality in terms shaped over 250 years ago. We now pay more attention to gender inequalities and to global (rather than just national) differences in wealth and income, but older ideas of equality of opportunity and the relation between natural and social inequalities (and increasingly, for obvious reasons, the political critique of obscenely excessive wealth) remain at the centre of thinking about these questions. In short, this book explains why social theory is an essential part of understanding the world.

Many of the thinkers discussed in this book defined themselves or were later defined as sociologists (the word 'sociology' was popularised in the 1830s by Auguste Comte – who also inaugurated the term 'positivism' to refer to the scientific study of nature and society – and came into general use in the early twentieth century), but social theory is a broader family, encompassing, for example, Hegel, Marx, Nietzsche, Foucault, perhaps Freud and certainly Frantz Fanon, Edward Said and other writers who shaped post-colonial theory. (The term 'social theory' was popularised in the UK in 1971 by Anthony Giddens, who reserved 'sociology' for more specific work emerging in the late nineteenth and early twentieth century that focused on industrial society.)

'YOU READ IT FIRST HERE': INNOVATIONS AND CONTINUITIES IN SOCIAL THEORY

'The privileged really come to consider themselves as a different species' – Abbé Sieyès

'The worst is when you have the poor to defend and the rich to contain' – Jean-Jacques Rousseau

These quotations do not come from a twenty-first-century social critic. The first is from 1788, the year before the outbreak of the French Revolution, and the second from a little earlier, in 1755. Our thinking about inequality, one of the topics of Chapter 1, is now focused once again on the ultra-rich, the '1%'. I will sketch the circumstances of then and now, showing how ideas that inspired revolution centuries ago remain powerfully relevant. Continuities of this kind run through social theory. The key innovation was the idea, which seems to have emerged in Europe and North America in the seventeenth and eighteenth centuries, that human societies can be understood as human products, shaped by underlying processes but also able to be reshaped by human intervention. The idea of 'knowing the causes of things' is much older (in Europe, the phrase goes back to the Roman poet Virgil, just before the Christian era), but the idea of the social as a distinct realm of reality is new.

Another novelty around this time was the idea of what we now call economic systems, operating according to their own laws but existing in and reshaping a social context. In the eighteenth century Adam Smith combined what we now think of as two very different areas of inquiry: economics and moral philosophy. (Not many people these days do both, though Amartya Sen is one of them.) For Karl Marx, a century after Smith, the emphasis had shifted to the analysis of capitalism as a system following its own laws and resistant to moral criticism. Marx also made the crucial link between classes and forms of production, in which positions in a system of production determine classes and the conflicts between them. Controversies around capitalism have been a central theme of social theory and are the topic of Chapter 2.

Chapter 3 examines the evolutionary sociology of Marx's contemporary (and his neighbour in Highgate Cemetery, north London) Herbert Spencer. Evolutionary theory was developed further in France by Emile Durkheim. Durkheim was one of the cluster of social theorists writing across the turn of the twentieth century who form the core of 'classical' social theory. His strong (some would say too strong) conception of society is a central reference point of modern social theory.

Chapter 4 returns to the theme of capitalism but focusing this time on its cultural preconditions and consequences. At the beginning of the twentieth century Max Weber traced what he thought was the crucial impact of a version of Protestant Christianity on the emergence of modern capitalism, and broadened this into a theory of 'rationalisation' expressed not just in *economic* calculation but also in legal and administrative systems, particularly bureaucracy, and religion itself (for example, in theology). Though they were contemporaries, Weber and Durkheim paid little attention to each other's work, but they form the two magnetic poles of classical social theory, with Weber's focus on the motivation of human action contrasted with Durkheim's stress on the determining quality of social influences.

The third of the leading classical theorists, Georg Simmel, who introduces Chapter 5, was closer to the Weberian pole. His most substantial work was also on the money economy, but his wide-ranging interests in cultural phenomena and everyday life inspired much ongoing work in sociology and cultural studies, including the 'postmodern' theory popular in the later twentieth century.

Chapter 6 departs from the classical *social* theorists and turns to Sigmund Freud, whose analysis of the psyche has fundamentally changed our understanding of humanity and hence culture and society. Are our social and political attitudes and actions shaped by underlying psychological influences? This chapter outlines Freud's work and traces its implications up to the present, through figures such as Herbert Marcuse, one of the thinkers who inspired the student and youth movements of the late 1960s.

Chapter 7 explores the ways in which some leading social theorists have tried to explain modern politics. Why are socialist parties so weak in the US? Why do the leaders of political parties, even socialist parties, become so detached from the mass of their members? Why did fascism achieve power in some European countries and not in others? I discuss the relation between the social and the political with these examples in mind.

The final chapter addresses some topics which have been rather neglected in social theory until fairly recently: gender, international relations and war, race and colonialism, and environmental crisis.

1

ORIGINS

This chapter focuses on the key questions posed by two early social theorists, Rousseau and Montesquieu, in the eighteenth century.

Jean-Jacques Rousseau wrote an essay in 1755 for a competition (which he didn't win) on the origins of inequalities in human societies. The term 'origins' should not be taken too literally, although he did refer to 'the first person who had the idea of enclosing a piece of land and saying "this is mine"'. We should, according to Rousseau, have rejected this claim, saying instead 'that the fruits of the earth belong to us all, and the earth itself to nobody'. This sounds like communism, but Rousseau's position was not quite so radical. He was concerned that social inequalities should not diverge too far from natural inequalities (strength, skill, etc.) and he was exceptionally hostile to luxury and excess. The essay concludes that 'it is plainly contrary to the law of nature, however defined, that children should command old men, fools wise men, and that the privileged few should gorge themselves with superfluities, while the starving multitude are in want of the bare necessities of life'.

Here are some of the central themes of social theory. One is the difference between the natural and the social, with the idea that, as Marx put it a century later, people make their own history but under given natural and historical conditions. The other is the distinction between moral and social criticism: Rousseau was a moralist but he also wanted to go beyond mere condemnation to offer explanations and diagnoses which could, as we would now say, inform policy. Some social theorists, notably Max Weber and Georg Simmel, see their role as merely to understand and explain (though Weber also produced highly polemical speeches and newspaper articles). Others, such as Marxists and feminists, offer an explicitly critical social theory.

Rousseau's critique of luxury and excess, and his idea that social inequalities should not be too great, and should not diverge too far from natural ones, is a theme which pervades later discussions, running from the sociologist and liberal politician Ralf Dahrendorf in the 1960s to Richard Wilkinson and Kate Pickett, Danny Dorling and Thomas Piketty today. Wilkinson and Pickett, in their influential book *The Spirit Level* (2009), showed that the more equal societies in the contemporary world are healthier and happier. Just what explains these differences remains unclear. One explanation is that levels of insecurity are higher in very unequal societies with poor welfare systems: in the US, for example, a short illness can mean financial disaster. Another, slightly more diffuse, explanation, which points forward to the discussion of Durkheim in Chapter 3, suggests that relatively equal societies have more of a common feeling of what Durkheim called solidarity and that this, rather than anything more tangible, may explain why they are healthier.

In France, Pierre Rosanvallon and Piketty have echoed and developed the Occupy movement's critique of the '1%', documenting the rise of inequality[1] and the way in which

the super-rich, as the Abbé Sieyès put it in 1788, see themselves as a different species. 'It is long past the time,' writes
Piketty, 'when we should have put the question of inequality
back at the center of economic analysis.' The explosion of
very high corporate salaries and related benefits is not just
a curiosity, like the similar rise in the incomes of professional footballers. In the corporate and financial world, it
contributed to the risky and corrupt practices which nearly
broke the world economy in 2008. As the British sociologist
Andrew Sayer neatly put it, 'We can't afford the rich.'

Perhaps, though, we need to look beyond these symptoms at the structure of capitalism; this has been one of the
main criticisms directed at Piketty's book. Chapter 2 opens
up these issues via a discussion of Karl Marx, for whom inequality was merely a symptom of the underlying problem:
wage labour under capitalism. A 'fairer' wage merely meant
that 'the length and weight of the golden chain the wage-
labourer has already forged for himself allow it to be loos-
ened somewhat'. As we have seen, Rousseau's preference
for the moderation of inequalities can be compared with
the more radical idea, popularised in Marxism, that people
should get what they need and contribute what they can to
society. Most recently, the very idea of 'natural' inequalities
– for example, of intelligence – long criticised on methodological grounds, has been questioned by advances in genet-
ics and performance-enhancing drugs. We now confront
the possibility that the rich may become smarter intellectu-
ally as well as in their clothing.

What, if anything, is wrong with inequality? So far we
have been looking at the question from two angles: the

attack on extremes of wealth and poverty and the idea that more equal societies seem to be healthier and perhaps happier. Somewhere in between are ideas of fairness and where trivial differences come to seem like major injustices. A British sociologist, W. G. Runciman, explored this issue in a book published in 1966 called *Relative Deprivation and Social Justice*. He found that people tend to compare themselves not with people who are much richer or poorer, but with people similar to themselves but a little better or worse off – for example, people paid more for working a night shift than during the day. Differences of this kind do not arouse concern, but differential pay for men and women (which used to be a common practice) is now illegal in much of the world.

Here we get to some interesting issues: should people who work hard get the same reward as those who don't? Systems of 'piecework' or 'performance-related pay' seem to reflect the idea that unequal rewards may be fairer. Interestingly, however, they are often rejected by employees. In vogue in the 1980s in the UK, they tended to be abandoned in the 1990s because they were seen as intrusive, divisive and not worth the trouble. Better perhaps to have a standard rate and rely on moral pressure to discourage slackers, rather as, at the end of a convivial meal, it may be better just to divide the bill than to get into the details of whether you ate or drank more than I did. In complex organisations, it's hard to evaluate individual contributions.

We have a mechanism which distributes money from a large number of people to a few: it's called a lottery and many people find it entertaining. What are the other mechanisms which generate inequality in our societies? Marx, as we shall see in the next chapter, identified the source of profit in capitalist economies in the fact that workers produce more value than they receive in wages. But more important in our societies are the power relationships in organisations which enable those at the top to set their rewards, justified of course by reference to the 'going rate' and a cult of 'leadership', whether for football managers or university vice-chancellors. Interestingly, the state socialist dictatorships of the twentieth century were not particularly egalitarian. In the Soviet Union, as in the West, a university professor might get three times the average salary, and top generals and academicians ten times. (There, of course, other privileges, such as access to scarce goods and resources, were in any case more important than cash.)

Anti-discrimination legislation gives another useful angle on these issues. When the UK legislated for equal pay for men and women in 1970, a number of employers tried to get round the Act by arguing that men and women were doing different work, where the differences were often trivial. The European Union legislation which trumped the UK Act used a broader principle of 'work of equal value'. There remains, however, a substantial gender pay gap, with wide variations across Europe.

Europe is also a good place to look at the interrelations of inequalities within and between countries. Inside member states, we tend to focus on domestic inequality, while the EU is more concerned with reducing inequalities between states; this is partly because stark inequalities encourage migration flows, which may cause short-term difficulties in social provision or fuel xenophobia in the native population. An interesting exercise which is rarely carried out is to put the two together: this shows, for example, that the richest fifth of the Romanian population had in 2012 a purchasing power roughly equal to that of the poorest fifth of Danes and twice that of the poorest fifth in Spain, while in crisis-ridden Greece the richest fifth were still close to the second-richest fifth in Germany and France.

Many economists used to believe that inequality is good for economic growth, because it provides incentives for hard work and investment. This sounds plausible enough, but, as so often, what seems to make sense at an individual level does not work at the level of whole societies or economies. Economic theory has now swung strongly behind the opposite view: that high levels of inequality reduce both opportunities and incentives for poorer individuals and households, discouraging them in particular from investing in education. Development theorists have long argued that supporting female education is a key to economic growth. Islamic fundamentalists may still reject this, but prosperity is probably not one of their priorities.

An important study published by the OECD at the end of 2014[2] traces the increase in inequality in the quarter-century before the economic crisis of the years since 2008 (which for the moment has halted the trend in some countries). In the mid-1980s the richest tenth of the population of OECD countries was on average seven times richer than the poorest tenth; by 2012 the ratio was nearly 10:1. In almost all these countries (mostly from the richer parts of the world, but including Mexico and Chile) inequality increased. This tends to reduce economic growth – for example, by discouraging poorer families (say, the lower 40 per cent) from investing in higher education. Britain and Israel, which are much more unequal than average, have low enrolments, though the US, which is even more unequal, has a much higher proportion in tertiary education, comparable to that in more equal European counties, such as Belgium and Denmark. (The quality of higher education in the US is, however, very variable, with some dodgy commercial 'universities'.) The OECD study estimates that the rise in inequality over the period cut growth by a fifth in the UK, the US and even the more equal countries of northern Europe. Its author stresses the need for remedial policies to focus on the bottom 40 per cent and not just on anti-poverty programmes.

Perhaps the main lesson to draw from all this is that our ideas of fairness and equality are historically shaped and highly variable. In the US, which is the fourth most unequal OECD country after Chile, Mexico and Turkey, taxation and welfare programmes do less to reduce inequality than in continental Europe, while US citizens are more likely to blame the poor for their condition. Even here, however, there has been widespread criticism of the 'top 1%', which may lead to more substantial changes in opinion. In Western Europe, where there is a more solid tradition of social democracy, protests have been more prominent – particularly, but not only, in the southern countries, where austerity has been most vicious and damaging. It may be that Rousseau and his contemporaries still have an important message in focusing on the moral dimension to their critique of excess. Calling them 'moralists' often carried a slightly dismissive tone, but this theme has again come to the fore in our own century. We may, however, ask, as we did in relation to Piketty, whether we need to go deeper to look at the roots of inequality in capitalist production.

In *The Social Contract* (1762) Rousseau asks another classic question of social theory: why 'man' is 'born free yet is everywhere in chains'. His democratic answer remains central to political thinking: that 'we the people' (the later American formulation) should agree to the laws we live under. Rousseau's distinction between the 'general will', concerned with the public good, and the aggregative 'will of all', based on individual interests, is highly relevant to modern politics – not least in the European Union. Have you ever seen a European politician come back from Brussels saying that the decision just taken is bad for the country but good for the Union as a whole, and that's really what matters? Something you might just about get away with in a national framework is out of the question in international or supranational politics.

Self-rule is the core idea of democracy, but it is also central to nationalist politics: if 'we the people' means Scots or Catalans, rather than Britons or Spaniards, national independence is on the agenda, as it was in Scotland in the 2014 referendum, which rejected independence by a rather narrow margin. If democracy and nationalism share the idea of self-rule, they may, however, also diverge. Fascists may destroy democracy in what they see as the national interest; democrats, including Rousseau, may be violently opposed to regional and other interest groups which they see as sectional.

We tend to think of democracy as an add-on to political liberalism, as in the standard phrase 'liberal democracy'; this reflects a fairly dominant pattern in Europe and its former colonies, where civil rights long preceded the extension of the vote to all adults. But democracies can also be highly illiberal; Rousseau was happy with the idea that people might have to be 'forced to be free'. Authoritarian regimes tend to use a democratic façade, even if there is only one party to vote for or opposition politicians are deprived of access to the media and are unusually prone to criminal prosecutions, car accidents and so on. Mexico under the Party of the Institutionalised Revolution (PRI) operated something like this second strategy in its seventy-one-year period of unbroken rule, as Russia does today.

Rousseau's contemporary Montesquieu might be called the father of modern social as well as political theory for his crucial intuition that political systems depend on a social context. Politics is, as it were, the visible part of a larger social iceberg. You can't choose in the abstract between democracy, monarchy and so on without asking how they will fit your society. In *The Spirit of Laws* (1748) he wrote that laws have to be understood in relation to 'the general spirit, customs and manners of a nation' and legislators have to take account of this: 'it is a very bad policy to change by laws what should be changed by manners'. Rousseau, in *The Social Contract*, compares the legislator to an architect who checks the ground to see if it will bear the weight of the planned building.

We no longer think, as Montesquieu did, that climate is an important factor in determining the suitability of political systems. (In hot climates, he wrote, people are timid like the elderly; in cold climates they are brave like the young. This is why, he thought, Asians and Africans put up with tyrannical empires which would not be accepted in Europe.) More promising is his idea that the geographical fragmentation of Europe, compared with the Eurasian steppes, has led to the emergence of a pattern of relatively small states and that this diversity is conducive to political liberty. This is an idea that continues to play a part in political histories of Europe: at the time of the Protestant Reformation, for example, it was handy if another state that practised and enforced your preferred version of Christianity was just a short journey away.

It is only recently that political leaders have been talking about (and not just attempting) 'regime change', but Montesquieu's analysis remains relevant. He had an acute awareness of the interplay between long-term structural causes and accidental events. While stressing the dependence of political and legal arrangements on broader social processes in what we would now call a holistic and multi-causal approach, he was conscious of the changeability of human laws and the influence of contingencies and 'past experiences'. This is a theme central to recent history and social theory under the heading of 'counterfactual conditionals'. For example:

1   If Hitler had died in the summer of 1939 the Second World War would not have taken place.

2   If Hitler had died in the summer of 1939 the Second World War would still have taken place.

Some historians discourage speculation of this sort, but the choice between 1 and 2 raises important questions about the role of individuals as opposed to larger structures in history. We can't turn back the clock; a number of people wished with hindsight that they had taken the opportunity to kill Hitler. The important question is, however, what difference this might have made to history.

Montesquieu also anticipated ideas of 'path dependence', which have been developed largely by economists and applied, for example, in discussions of post-communist transition and 'varieties of capitalism'. There may be various possible routes from A to B, but once you've chosen a route it's usually better to stick to it. The 'qwerty' layout of the keyboard on which I'm typing this sentence may not be the most convenient arrangement of the letters, but once it's established it would be crazy to try to implement an alternative. There are various possible ways in which people could have reintroduced capitalism and democracy in post-communist Europe, but choices made in the first few weeks will tend to constrain options later on. Which is better, a liberal market economy like those in the US and UK or a more coordinated one like Germany's, where banking finance plays a bigger role and corporations are less short-termist in their decision-making? The answer may depend on where you're starting from.

Montesquieu's idea of 'the general spirit' of a nation is central to the approach taken by the liberal French aristocrat Alexis de Tocqueville in his book *Democracy in America*, based on a tour of the US in 1831–2, and published in two volumes in 1835 and 1840. Tocqueville showed how the success of American republican representative democracy is grounded in what he calls 'equality of conditions', in a society without an aristocracy or monarchy (though of course with slavery in the South and racism also in the North). However, democracy in this broad sense, which he saw as the future for France, also brought with it dangers of conformism and what he called, in a phrase that has stuck, the 'tyranny of the majority'. Montesquieu's idea is also echoed in what Durkheim later called the 'collective consciousness'; Durkheim in fact wrote substantially about Montesquieu and Rousseau as precursors of sociology (see Further Reading). We can't, I think, talk about either of them as launching a paradigm in the sense of a structured framework of assumptions or what Kuhn called a 'disciplinary matrix', but both were major innovators in the way they addressed issues of inequality, democracy and the relation between the social and the political.

2

CAPITALISM

Like it or not, capitalism has fundamentally shaped Western life for the past few centuries, and now shapes the lives of most people in the world. With the demise of the Soviet empire in 1989–91, and the changes in China since then, it has become a near-universal economic and social form. Cuba and North Korea are still notionally communist, but maybe not for much longer. Marx's analysis remains one of the most powerful ways of thinking about capitalism. Marx and his collaborator Friedrich Engels used the language of natural science to describe their thinking: Marx wrote of the commodity as the 'cell-form' of capitalism and of capturing its 'laws of motion'. Engels's speech at Marx's funeral described him as having discovered the laws of social evolution, just as Darwin had discovered those of natural evolution. Marx had himself pointed out that he had not of course *discovered* the existence of classes, but his idea that forms of production and class antagonisms based on them shape modern societies remains a key strand in contemporary social theory.

Let us start, as Marx began *Capital* in 1867, with commodities or goods. A commodity, such as the computer I am using to write this book, has what Marx called 'use value': you can do things with it. It also has what he called 'exchange value': I could try to exchange it for something else or sell it for cash. Marx drew on his anthropological reading in his analysis of what he called the 'fetishism' of commodities, in which they take on a magical quality almost like objects of worship. A designer handbag, for example, has a 'wow factor' and seems to be 'worth' more, irrespective of the cost of the materials and labour that went into its production. As Marx put it, a social relation between people takes on the form of a relation between things: 1 Gucci bag = 10 Primark ones. The term 'reification' (turning a human relation into a thing) came into use later, but it captures the idea very well.

An exchange economy really gets going when people don't just use money as what Marx called the 'universal equivalent', a convenient way of mediating the exchange of one thing for another, but buy things in order to resell them at a profit. What Marx called 'labour-power', the capacity of humans to work, can also be a commodity under capitalism. You can hire someone at, say, £30 an hour to fix your computer if it goes wrong. Capitalists systematically employ workers to produce goods and services which they (hope to) sell at a profit. Where does profit come from? Basically, according to Marx, from the fact that wage workers produce more value than they get back in their wages; he called this 'surplus value'. Any additional profit or loss resulting from, for example, market fluctuations in supply and demand or skill or luck at producing a successful product is secondary to this basic process. The exploitation of wage labour, in other words, is not a regrettable feature of nasty forms of capitalism: it is intrinsic to the process.

So is the conflict of interests between workers and capitalists. Workers have to work for capitalists in order to live, as independent agricultural or artisanal work is squeezed out by more 'efficient' capitalist forms. They can't realistically demand the 'full value of their labour', as some socialists did in Marx's time, since this would be incompatible with the survival of capitalism. In Britain, the famous 'Clause Four' of the Labour Party constitution, introduced in 1918 (and printed on the back of party membership cards) and removed by Tony Blair in 1995, recognised this connection in stating its aim: 'To secure for the workers by hand or by brain the full fruits of their industry and the most equitable distribution thereof that may be possible upon the basis of the common ownership of the means of production, distribution and exchange . . .'

Marx's 'labour theory of value' has been heavily criticised, both at the time and as capitalist production became more automated. Although Marx devoted a lot of his analysis to the introduction of machinery and what he called the change in the 'organic composition of capital', many later commentators have concluded that this actually breaks the model apart. A worker in a highly automated plant can 'earn' his or her week's wages in a few minutes' work, and it seems artificial to describe the capital equipment s/he uses just as 'stored-up labour'. But the basic idea that capitalists grow rich at the expense of the rest of the population may survive these theoretical difficulties. Tocqueville too had noted in a Manchester factory that 'labour-saving devices are constantly being invented and, by increasing the competition among the workers, bring down the level of wages'.

Capitalism, in Marx's analysis, generates class conflict, which is the fundamental conflict in modern societies and possibly, as Marx and Engels claimed in *The Communist Manifesto* (1848), in other forms of society as well. The conflict of interests is obscured by what they called 'ideology': in this case, in particular, the ideology of a fair day's pay for a fair day's work. Workers who are paid 'the rate for the job' don't realise they're being exploited. There are also other forms of ideology saying something like, in the British prime minister David Cameron's phrase, 'We're all in this together.' Against this idea of a national community or other non-class 'communities', such as those of religious believers, ethnic groups and so on, Marxism urges international class struggle by the 'workers of all countries' against global capitalism.

Marxism, unlike the other social theories discussed in this book, is of course still a major political force outside the academy. We need to look first at the plausibility of the Marxist claim that forms of production fundamentally shape other aspects of social life and human history before asking whether capitalism is now 'the only game in town'.

Marx and Engels tend to use a rather weak argument that because the production and reproduction of material life is fundamental to the survival of human societies it therefore determines their structure. In Marx's pithy summary, 'The hand-mill gives you society with the feudal lord; the steam-mill society with the industrial capitalist.' (This is what we now call 'technological determinism' and it will recur from time to time in the rest of this book.) In practice, Marx's position is a good deal more sensitive to social diversity, and he once said that he 'wasn't a Marxist'. Whether his production-focused approach is appropriate to, for example, hunter-gatherer societies is a complex issue which I shall not address here, but Marx was certainly interested in it and compiled a number of ethnographical notebooks documenting his reading. Capitalism was, however, his main concern, and he studied it in one of its most advanced forms, in Britain, where he and Engels had settled after the failure of the 1848 revolutions. A little earlier, Engels in 1844 and Tocqueville in 1835 had described the conditions of the working class in Manchester in very similar terms, differing only in their proposed remedies. Tocqueville suggested reforms, involving a better regulation of industrialisation and of migration into the industrial towns, and a more equitable sharing out of the benefits of prosperity. For the young Engels, as early as 1844, the remedy was communism: 'The revolution must come.'

The most fundamental criticisms of Marx's model, as well as those focused on his labour theory of value, concern the way he downplayed the role of political and legal structures in his distinction between economic 'base' and political 'superstructure'. He had intended to write in detail about the state in later volumes of *Capital* but his early death meant that this, like the editing of Volumes 2 and 3 of *Capital*, was left to Engels, who commented that he and Marx had over-emphasised the primacy of the productive base. They were also very vague about what politics would look like under communism: if the state is essentially an instrument of rule by the dominant class, it loses its importance in a class-less society and politics becomes just a matter of rational democratic decision-making. Feminists and other critics have pointed out that there is more to politics than class.

We tend to think of Marxism as a very political theory compared with the others discussed in this book, and in some ways this is obviously true. But it also rather naively envisages a future 'end to politics'.

Marx, unlike Rousseau and Montesquieu, can unquestionably be seen as founding a paradigm in Kuhn's sense. Many social theorists are happy to describe themselves as Marxists, and many more would cite Marx and Marxism as the key reference point for their own work. There is even a slightly unhealthy tendency to describe developments which differ from Marx as 'what he really meant', or what the mature Marx really thought, rather than accepting that any thinker's views change over time and may need to be revised. 'Revisionism' has always been a dirty word among more orthodox Marxists, and the fact that we speak of 'orthodoxy', as with Judaism or Christianity, is disturbing in a tradition which is essentially atheistic. (Some brilliant thinkers, such as the literary theorist Terry Eagleton or the philosopher Andrew Collier, have tried to combine Marxism and religion, and there is a whole tradition of liberation theology which is often Marxist, but there is clearly a tension between the two components.)

The Italian Marxist theorist and interwar communist activist Antonio Gramsci developed Marx's model with his attention to what he called civil society and hegemony and the differences between Russia and the rest of Europe. In imperial Russia, 'the state was everything', and independent social organisations barely existed except in the big cities. In Italy and other similar societies, there were active non-state bodies and an independent public sphere. This meant that socialists in Italy in the 1920s could not aim simply to capture the state in a single revolutionary act, but had to reshape the 'common sense' of the society and win over a substantial part of civil society.

Marx and Engels had themselves pointed the way here in their analysis of ideology. In an unpublished book, *The German Ideology*, which has become (in abridged versions) one of the classic Marxist texts, they addressed the fundamental question of the importance of ideas in human history. The German socialists they criticised there overstressed the role of ideas, believing that criticism was enough on its own to transform reality. For Marx and Engels, false ideas, such as the idea of a fair day's pay mentioned above, emerge from forms of production and the political and legal relations corresponding to them. These had to be tackled directly in practical action, though also by critical social analysis of the kind Marx later provided in *Capital*.

One of Marx's starting points, in addition to the criticism of contemporary social injustices, had been the critique of religion. Voltaire had said that if God made man in His own image, man had 'certainly returned the compliment'. Ludwig Feuerbach, whom Marx described as 'the true conqueror of the old philosophy', later developed this idea of religion as a human projection in more detail. Marx took the falsity of religion for granted and asked *why* people believed in it. His famous phrase about religion as 'the opium of the people' was preceded by the less often quoted description of it as 'the sigh of the oppressed creature, the heart of a heartless world'. We take refuge in the illusions of religion because our social and political conditions are unsatisfactory.

In particular, the political sphere is an imitation of the religious sphere, with the same rituals and mumbo-jumbo. And why is the political sphere like this? Because our social relations are also torn apart by exploitation and class antagonisms. The idealist philosopher Hegel believed that the state could reconcile these social antagonisms; Marx said you needed a social and not just a political revolution. People are not intrinsically antagonistic. The estrangement of people from one another in market societies is reflected in the separation between state and society and between politics and religion. So if you pull at the thread of religion, as Marx did, you'll pull apart, at least in theory, the rest of the sweater of capitalist society, including sweated labour.

All this means that ideology is not just a by-product of social relations. Ideas, Marx said later, 'become a practical force when they seize the masses'. So it matters if things appear in a distorted form. Marx used the image of the camera obscura, where things outside appear upside down. In ideology, for example, God appoints the monarch, who looks after society; our duty is to worship God and respect the monarch. In capitalism, the 'rate for the job' obscures the extraction of surplus value, justifying exploitation in a form of ideology which is more subtle than the feudal landlord demanding part of your produce because of your place in the God-given hierarchy. (You notice if your landlord takes one of your four bales of hay, whereas your payslip doesn't show a deduction for capitalist profit.) Both in Marx's time and since, analyses of ideology have suggested that it also legitimates inequalities and exploitation based on gender, ethnicity and so on.

Gramsci took the term 'hegemony' from Lenin, who had used it to refer to the leadership of the Russian working class over the much more numerous peasantry in the Russian Revolution. Gramsci made it the starting point for his analysis of the way in which the Italian working class, operating in a much more open ideological political context, might mobilise the support of other parts of Italian society. His ideas were exceptionally influential elsewhere in Western Europe, particularly the UK, in the second half of the twentieth century. They were taken up by the British Marxist journal *New Left Review* and were central to the thought of one of the most brilliant sociologists of the period, and a founder of cultural studies (as well as of *New Left Review*), Stuart Hall. Hall coined the term 'Thatcherism' and was one of the most acute analysts of the way in which Mrs Thatcher combined neoliberal economic dogma, a populist style of politics and a more traditional nationalistic (and even xenophobic) conservatism in a powerful synthesis.

Is there something about economic life which means that it is best organised on the basis of markets? Marx thought not. At least in his early work, he contrasted a hypothetical situation in which people work to satisfy other people's needs, as parents or family carers typically do in our own societies, with what he called alienated or 'estranged' labour for a market, where work is merely a means to an end. It is this that makes even independent work alienated; if the capitalist controls the production process, as in much mechanised or assembly-line work, this is just an additional element of alienation. Money, as opposed to more informal forms of reciprocity or exchange, may denature social relations. (As the author Jeanette Winterson once said, just try giving your lover a £20 note the morning after a night of passion.)

Other analysts, both long before and long after Marx, have disagreed with this approach. Adam Smith famously wrote that 'It is not from the benevolence of the butcher, the brewer, or the baker that we expect our dinner, but from their regard to their own interest.' What's wrong with this? 'Rational action theory' would say that this is just the way we are, though some would say that we can also choose to devote ourselves to selfless work for others. Any alternative to market production also raises the question of information. A centrally planned economy like that of the Soviet Union relied on predictions of what goods would be needed and what could be produced but suffered notoriously from shortages. A market made up of independent producers can respond more flexibly to changes in demand. On the other hand, there are some goods, such as health care, which we may feel should not be commodified and marketed; a hospital that refuses you emergency treatment because your credit card is out of date seems to violate important principles.

Another set of questions concerns the control of capitalism. Many states allow the buying and selling of land, including small islands, but would worry if, say, the privately owned Channel Island of Brecqhou, adjacent to Sark, was sold to a Russian, as the Greek island of Skorpios was in 2013. More seriously, capitalist interests can effectively control states – most dramatically in the case of 'narco-states'. (There is a substantial overlap between legal and illegal enterprise, as shown by discussion of the prospective legalisation of currently illegal drugs.)

Social democrats tried to square the circle by having the state control what Labour in Britain called the 'commanding heights' of the economy, leaving the rest in private hands. The more fashionable alternative is to introduce private ownership of even essential infrastructure and utilities, but with some form of governmental 'regulation' to stop things getting out of hand. (When I first played Monopoly, in the 1960s, I thought the idea that you could buy or sell utility companies was a quaint bit of ancient history . . .)

Stepping back from these current controversies, we might ask, as sociologists did in the mid-twentieth century, whether what really made a difference was industrialism rather than capitalism. This was the age of the cold war, beginning in 1947, with West and East coolly contemplating nuclear Armageddon and basing deterrence on 'mutually assured destruction', often abbreviated to MAD. One of the few sociologists who paid serious attention to these issues, Raymond Aron, is better known for his theorisation of what he called 'industrial society'. Aron pointed to the similarities between the developed capitalist and socialist societies which were lined up against each other. Both were substantially devoted to large-scale industrial production (sometimes called Fordism after Henry Ford's massive car plants), with populations increasingly living in cities, highly educated and reliant on complex transportation systems (cars, urban railroads, etc.). Moscow had no private shops and far fewer private cars than New York, but its basic infrastructure and demographic structure were pretty much the same.

The next step, though it was one which Aron resisted, was the theory of 'convergence': that these similarities between the two types of society would become greater. In an approach known as 'functionalism' (discussed in more detail in the next chapter), where institutions such as families and educational systems are explained by their beneficial consequences for society as a whole, the logic of industrialism *required* people to be educated, urban, healthy, mobile and so on. (This is a non-Marxist version of 'technological determinism', where technology determines social relations.) A good way of thinking about this approach is in something like the image of concentric circles shown here, which I remember the sociologist of development Ron Dore using in a lecture many years ago.

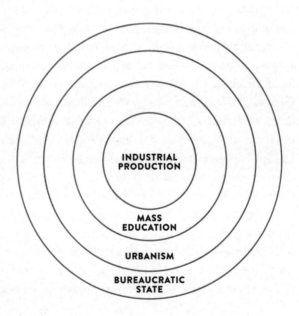

INDUSTRIAL
PRODUCTION

MASS
EDUCATION

URBANISM

BUREAUCRATIC
STATE

The inner circle of industrial production, focused on steel, coal, oil, electricity generation and so on, and taking a similar form on both sides of the Iron Curtain, is surrounded by other circles of demographic structures, family patterns, urban settlement, universal education and so on. You don't need to rear a big family if you can be fairly sure that your children will survive and you don't have a family farm; you do, however, need to live in big towns where large-scale industry is mostly located, and people may need to be able to read and write (and count) to do this sort of work. Part of the motivation behind the Soviet Union's crash programme of industrialisation in the 1930s was the belief that an educated, skilled working class would support Soviet power. A powerful industrial state would also protect the USSR in case of another war – as it did when Hitler attacked in 1941.

Convergence theory contradicted the official ideologies of the two forms of society, according to which the USSR and its satellites were totalitarian dictatorships or, alternatively, the US and similar societies were not just exploitative but also warlike. It was, however, compatible with the idea that communism, far from being an advance on capitalism, was an avoidable accident, a 'disease of the transition' to industrial society, when the strains of industrialisation might provide an opportunity for socialist agitators to foment and profit from discontent.

In 1989, when the communist dictatorships collapsed in Eastern Europe, and in 1991, when the Soviet Union dissolved itself, it did indeed look as though communism had been, as an old joke put it, the longest route from capitalism to capitalism, though communist movements and even some regimes survived elsewhere. (China squared the circle, preserving a Communist Party dictatorship but introducing a substantially capitalist economy.) In the West, Marxist theory had always been one social theory among others, tending to blend with the other theory families discussed in later chapters, and the Marxist emphasis on class conflict had been taken up in non-Marxist theories of democratic politics. In Europe, though not in the US, political competition tended to involve a party or parties with working-class support and a more or less socialist ideology, opposed by conservative and liberal parties.

In the last third of the twentieth century, anti-capitalist movements combined, as well as competed, with 'new social movements' in addressing issues on which socialism had had rather little to say: gender inequality, the politics of lifestyles and the developing environmental crisis, which was already an issue of concern. The emancipation of women from patriarchy (the rule of fathers and men) had been one focus among others of socialist political theory, as in Engels's book *The Origin of the Family, Private Property and the State* (1884) and in the work and practice of Isaac Bebel in imperial Germany and Alexandra Kollontai in revolutionary Russia. Towards the end of the twentieth century, socialist feminists confronted the interplay of capitalist relations of production and patriarchal relations of reproduction and domestic labour. Others followed the US feminist Betty Friedan in rewriting the slogan of *The Communist Manifesto* to read that the history of all societies so far has been the history of a gender struggle between men and women.

Marxism was against the exploitation of humans but did not bother much about the exploitation of nature, seeing it as potentially offering progress and prosperity for all. Gradually, however, the political Left took up issues of the dangers of excessive growth, the loss of animal species and environmental risk. Ulrich Beck's book *Risk Society* came out in 1986, closely followed by the accident at the Chernobyl nuclear power plant in Ukraine which contaminated Europe as far as Wales, and Asia as far as the Pacific, and could easily have been much more serious.

Whereas there are strong elements of feminism in the thought of Marx and Engels (and Marx's daughter Eleanor was a pioneer of what came to be called Marxist feminism), there is not much prospect of reconstructing a 'green' Marx. There is, however, in Marx's thinking a strong emphasis on the location of humans in nature and the need for a harmonious relationship with (the rest of) nature, and it is certainly possible to argue that only socialism can provide the conditions for the sustainable development of human societies.

3

SOCIETY

Opposite Marx's grave in Highgate Cemetery is that of Herbert Spencer, one of the first people after Auguste Comte to call himself a sociologist, and the pioneer of evolutionary social theory. Spencer drew on the image of human societies as organisms, with government as the brain, transport networks as nerves, veins and so on, and an overall process of social development corresponding to natural evolution and leading to a shift in human societies from militaristic to industrial forms – anticipating the theory of industrial society discussed in the previous chapter. Evolutionary social theory has had something of a revival in recent years. It's the equivalent of Marmite in social theory: people are divided between those who think it's the only way to make social theory scientific and those who violently reject it.

One of the core ideas of evolutionary social theory is differentiation. Natural evolution runs from single-cell organisms to humans and other 'higher' animals. Societies can also be seen as developing from 'simple' forms, in which most people do one or two sorts of thing (child-rearing, hunting and gathering food, etc.) to modern societies, where a list of occupations can run into thousands. Some Western critics of communist societies focused on their lack of differentiation and enforced ideological conformism, making them poorer at certain forms of innovation, such as computing, in the later twentieth century.

Another strand of social evolutionary theory focuses not so much on differentiation as on learning. This is closer to Comte's idea that human thought, and the individual sciences, move from a theological stage, in which phenomena are explained by supernatural forces, through a metaphysical stage of explanations in terms of abstract principles, to a positive stage of precise scientific demonstration based on observation and experimentation. Mathematics, physics and biology had made this transition and sociology, the queen of the sciences, was now completing it in the work of Comte himself. This conception, though not Comte's subsequent invention of a 'religion of humanity', was taken up enthusiastically by philosophers such as John Stuart Mill and by some historians. Shortly after, it was an important influence on Durkheim's idea of a scientific sociology. In the later twentieth century, the notion of evolutionary learning was used by Jürgen Habermas in his 'reconstruction' of Marx's historical materialism.

More problematic in the transfer of evolutionary ideas from nature to society is the idea of natural selection or the 'survival of the fittest'. Did the Allies win the two world wars of the twentieth century because they were 'fitter' or for other reasons? Can the collapse of societies be explained so simply? Most attempts to explain 'collapse', such as Jared Diamond's influential book of 2005 with that title, stress a multiplicity of different factors. To explain the collapse of communism in Europe, for example, you need to examine a whole bundle of elements, ranging from inefficiencies in the economic planning system to the changing international role of the Soviet Union, ideological disillusionment and probably also the corrosive effect of Western rock music and pop culture. We tend to write the history of both nature and human societies so that things appear inevitable, whereas in fact there were lots of alternative possibilities at every stage. Recent research suggests that the extinction of the dinosaurs was (for them) an unfortunate accident. What if they had survived? Would we be here now? The theories of path dependence mentioned in Chapter 1 in relation to Montesquieu are careful to avoid suggesting that we always start on the best path.

Organisms have operating parameters: if my temperature soars to abnormal levels I know to consult a doctor. We sometimes call societies 'sick' or 'healthy', but we lack the equivalent of a thermometer or a scanner. Should we even be thinking about societies in this way, and what are they anyway? By the end of the nineteenth century organic analogies were becoming less popular, but Emile Durkheim continued something like an evolutionary approach with his contrast between the 'mechanical solidarity' of tribal societies, where people have a sense of commonality because they are all hunter-gatherers doing much the same things, and the 'organic solidarity' of societies with a more developed division of labour. In societies of this second type, we depend on one another for goods and services, as Adam Smith and Spencer had recognised. Durkheim diverged from Spencer, however, in stressing the need for solidarity and shared ideas to cement these interdependencies.

Durkheim also believed that by looking at native

Australian totemism, in which human groups were associated with natural objects or animals, he could identify the 'elementary forms of religious life'. All religions, he argued, distinguish between sacred and non-sacred things; even secularists may think of human rights or state boundaries as sacred. Religion is too pervasive in human societies to be just a mistake, so if it's not about a supernatural or spiritual world it must be really about society. There *is* something outside ourselves, bigger than we are, present long before we were born and surviving (we assume) long after our deaths, which gives meaning to our lives. Misidentified by religious believers as something supernatural, it is actually the societies in which we live. Religions, and even secular belief systems, celebrate society and social solidarity.

Durkheim's theory of religion illustrates an important feature of social theory. If you were a religious believer when you began to read the previous paragraph, and if you accept (rather briskly) the argument summarised in it, you may by now have ceased to be a believer. Marx similarly started from the assumption that religious belief was mistaken in order to unravel the forms of human and social and political life which give rise to, among other things, religious illusions. We imagine an ideal world because our own world is, as he put it, 'heartless'; we imagine an ideal and benevolent ruler of the world because our own rulers are not all they might be, though we also dress up politics in religious language and imagery and we may assume, as Hegel did, according to Marx, that politics can heal the conflicts in our societies, bringing us all together, as in a church, in the service of the common good. Religion and politics, for Marx, are estranged or alienated expressions of something wrong in our societies: the exploitation of some humans by others.

Some social theories have this 'unmasking' quality; others may reinforce or at least not challenge conventional beliefs. Evolutionary theory tends to reassure us that things have turned out OK after all, leaving us with just a few residues (such as the appendix used to be believed to be), which we no longer need but can be removed if they cause trouble. Closely linked to evolutionism is a social theory very prominent in the mid-twentieth century known as functionalism, which Durkheim anticipated in his first major book, on the division of labour. The basic idea, and an unproblematic one, is the question: what does [some natural or social object] *do*? The heart pumps blood around the body; families provide a basis for kinship relations and, very often, the rearing of children. To say this is not to say, unless you believe in a divine creator, that they were put in place with that intention, but it is *as if* they were. If your heart rhythm is disturbed, you can install various bits of deliberately designed equipment to improve its operation. Similarly, although human family structures evolved from those of other apes, humans often intervene to 'support' the family, by financial or legal means or policies to encourage reproduction.

Functions are usually seen as useful. Durkheim argued that the division of labour performed a beneficial function, generating an 'organic solidarity' arising from relations of interdependence, though this was not what explained its emergence. This he explained by a growth in the density of human societies and people's desire to find a niche where they were not competing with others doing the same thing as themselves.

Functionalism also argues that, for example, economic rewards and other forms of social recognition correspond to our contribution to society and that inequalities are required to motivate people to make exceptionally valuable contributions (such as running banks into the ground). While this justificatory approach is a natural consequence of functionalism (though it also addresses malfunctions or 'dysfunctions'), Marxism could also be used in 'communist' societies to reassure you that everything was for the best and that you were lucky not to be living in the capitalist West. A classic book by the US sociologist Alvin Gouldner, *The Coming Crisis of Western Sociology* (1970), pointed to these parallels between North American functionalism and Soviet Marxism.

This idea of societies holding together, of social health or sickness, also underlay Durkheim's best-known book, *Suicide* (1897), in which he argued that social variables (marital status, religion, etc.) explained differences in suicide rates. Protestant Christian populations, he suggested, had higher rates than Catholics because they were less closely integrated. Protestantism encourages independent reflection, which may weaken the force of shared beliefs. Catholics also had close contact with a priest (sometimes too close, we might now say after so many accounts of sexual abuse) and rituals of confession and absolution, whereas Protestants had a lonelier relationship with an absent god. Single people were on the whole more prone to suicide than married people, again suggesting the importance of social ties.

Stressing the need for social integration, Durkheim suggested that one could distinguish between 'normal' and 'pathological' states of society. A 'normal' rate of crime or suicide is what is statistically normal for a society of that type (for example, modern industrial societies such as France or Germany). Where rates are abnormally high or low, we ask why. For him, society is an explanatory principle: it explains, for example, our moral codes. What counts as bad behaviour in a monastic community will be very different from what is condemned in a criminal gang; Durkheim's approach is in that sense relativistic, while making a rather bold claim for the possibility of objective sociological diagnosis.

Durkheim's analysis of suicide continues to be a major focus of contemporary research, as Christian Baudelot and Roger Establet show in their book *Suicide: The Hidden Side of Modernity* (2008). Durkheim's basic stress on social integration as a protection against suicide is correct, they argue, but it needs to be understood in a more nuanced way. He was wrong, for example, simply to say that poverty protects us from suicide. In thinking about poverty, we need to differentiate between poverty as a shared condition of pretty much a whole population and the kind of poverty that, especially in richer societies, means disqualification, loss of respect and social exclusion. It is the latter that probably explains higher suicide rates among poorer people or districts.

Durkheim's sociology of religion also offers what has come to be called a 'sociology of knowledge', since the structure of society explains not only our religious beliefs but our scientific and cultural beliefs as well. Focusing again on what he thought of as simple or 'primitive' societies, Durkheim and his sociologist nephew, Marcel Mauss, argued that the spatial structure of settlements tended to be replicated in conceptions of the heavens. Our basic ideas of time and space are shaped by social time (seasons, harvests, festivals, etc.) and social space (for example, where our settlement ends and the next one begins).

Durkheim's analysis of belief systems contrasts with what Marxists and others call 'ideology', where the themes of distortion, false consciousness and unmasking are stronger. For Durkheim, the main contrast is between common-sense knowledge and the scientific knowledge of the sociologist. Class conflict resulted from a pathological state of the division of labour. It was not intrinsic to capitalism and could be reduced by abolishing the inheritance of property and by the development of occupational corporations linking workers and employers, like the medieval guilds.

Durkheim's use of social statistics is a good example of a paradigmatic innovation in social theory. Even if his statistics were unreliable (as they were) and his inferences often dubious and arbitrary, sociologists still use him as a reference point. The 'Durkheimian School', which was once so strong in France, has long since disappeared, but there is still something like a recognisable Durkheimian approach within social theory. Durkheim's strong conception of society and his stress on social solidarity and shared value systems were taken up in the mid-twentieth century in functionalist sociology and system theory. Other functionalist Ideas of cybernetics, feedback and equilibrium were applied to human societies and to economic and political systems. Economic models became particularly fashionable. (In the days before computers, for example, the UK Treasury had a hydraulic model of the British economy; unfortunately it leaked on the floor.)

In a brilliant commentary on system theory, the British sociologist David Lockwood pointed out that it ran together two forms of integration which should be distinguished: system integration (how well the parts of the system fit together) and social integration (how well the people who make up the system relate to one another). This contrast can be seen in use, for example, in proposals for the reform of the European Union, with some analysts stressing the reshaping of EU institutions and others emphasising the need to encourage the development of a stronger sense of European identity and solidarity among political leaders and populations.

Durkheim, unlike some later functionalist theorists, was careful to distinguish between the functions of a social institution, such as the division of labour, and the causes that brought it about. To say something exists because it is beneficial to society only explains it if you can demonstrate some mechanism by which these beneficial consequences are realised. This might be a semi-automatic feedback mechanism, as in a gyroscope, or it might be through deliberate policy, as when politicians try to strengthen 'the family' because they believe it is beneficial to society. More fundamentally, however, the whole system model can be questioned by people who deny that societies hang together in this way and prefer to focus on individual action. As we shall see in the next chapter, Durkheim's contemporary Max Weber rejected organic models of society in favour of an interpretive sociology of social action. I argued in a book of 2006 that this is a more defensible position, especially as modern societies become less bounded and more fragmented as a result of globalisation, international migration, the formation of transnational political associations like the European Union and so on.

4

ORIGINS OF CAPITALISM AND THEORIES
OF SOCIAL ACTION

Who cares where capitalism came from? Marx certainly did, though he tended to stress the present: 'The anatomy of man,' he wrote, 'is a key to the anatomy of the ape.' But it *does* make a difference, not least to modern post-colonial theory, whether we see the emergence of capitalism as a 'European miracle' (the title of Eric Jones's influential book of 1981) or rather as a reconfiguration of *global* relations of production, trade and military conquest in which different world regions rise and fall. Europe's greater prominence in the second half of the last millennium was partly the result of changes in previously more advanced world regions. Now, once again, Europeans are looking east for examples of cutting-edge technology.

Max Weber, who worked first in economic history but came to identify himself as a sociologist, has been called the bourgeois Marx. His approach is one of the other main strands of modern social theory. Weber, though an intensely political animal, was committed to 'value-free' social science and the separation of factual analysis and evaluation. He took the politics out of Marxist analysis, modified Marx's class model and developed an idea of social action which grew into the interpretive social theory discussed below.

While Marxism was one of Weber's reference points,

perhaps his most-read work, *The Protestant Ethic and the Spirit of Capitalism* (1904–5), suggests a counter-model to Marxism, though he admits it would be 'equally one-sided' if taken as the whole truth. Instead of assuming, as Marx had, that forms of production (in this case, early capitalism) give rise to ideologies which justify them (such as Protestant Christianity, emerging at the same time), Weber asks if we could turn the question round. What if the Protestant 'work ethic', which had religious origins, gave a kick-start to the more 'rational' forms of capitalism which, he believed, were established earlier in the parts of Europe that had adopted Calvinist Protestantism? He thought it did, and much of his later work was devoted to showing how other major world religions (Judaism, Islam, Hinduism, Buddhism, Confucianism and Taoism) had not played this role in places where the early emergence of modern capitalism had also been a possibility.

The relevance of this goes far beyond a historical controversy. Weber was also analysing the emergence of a modern bourgeois way of life, rationally self-interested and calculating, though coexisting with a commitment to other moral, religious or political values – the characteristics of Western and, increasingly, global modernity. Social theory as Weber developed it aimed to understand as well as to explain human conduct, where Marx had tended to see it as a simple product of social relations. Marx thought it was obvious that capitalists had to accumulate profit, whereas Weber wanted to know how people made sense of this new idea of systematically calculating and measuring it.

The idea of understanding people's actions 'from the

inside' had been a strong theme in German historical writing in the late nineteenth century, but it was Weber and Simmel who introduced it into sociology. Human actions (and those of other animals), if they are not just involuntary, have a 'meaning' that natural processes do not. We may say that black clouds 'mean' rain and that the rain 'means' that the river will flood, but these are not intentional or otherwise meaningful processes in the way that I 'mean' to finish my book or that *Buch* 'means' book in German. We can understand, in the sense of explain, how the Thames cut a path down to the place we now call London, but the growth of the city can also be understood in terms of the purposes of the people who settled there on the banks of the river.

One form of this understanding may consist of sympathy or empathy, but another is simply the feeling that behaviour 'makes sense', as when neighbours say that they did not sell their house because they did not get a good enough offer. In Weber's model of the Protestant economic ethic, people who were worried about their salvation looked for reassurance in the fact that their hard work in their 'calling' was producing satisfactory results. For Weber, this 'made sense'; he gathered some (rather sketchy) evidence that people did think this way and some controversial economic statistics suggesting that Calvinist Protestant parts of early modern Europe were economically more innovative than regions which had remained Catholic. His tentative explanation was both 'meaningfully adequate' and 'causally adequate'.

'Rubbish,' Durkheim might have said if he had read *The Protestant Ethic*. (As far as we know, he didn't.) 'Stick to what can be observed and measured and don't make conjectures about intentions and other mental processes.' In fact, however, Durkheim's *Suicide* is full of common-sense ideas about 'what it is like' to be widowed, divorced or whatever. Despite his insistence that scientific sociology should break with common sense, he relies on it as much as Weber.

In Weber's developed system, published after his early death in 1920, he identifies four main types of action, to which our actual actions may conform more or less closely. Traditional action is mostly unreflective; if we are asked to explain why we act in a certain way we simply say 'habit' or 'that's the way we do it here'. Outsiders can understand this, even if they think the practice is 'primitive' or silly. Emotionally driven action, such as the 'road rage' that causes us to hoot or make rude signs, is usually also unreflective. Again, we can understand it, even if we think it excessive, as when people are attacked for giving someone a 'funny look'. Then there are two types of what Weber calls rational action. The first is purposive-rational, where we adopt what we think is the best means to achieve a given purpose. If there are no satisfactory means, as with a journey which can't be completed in the time available, we give up. In the second form of rational action, which Weber calls value-rational, we pursue the value whatever the cost. Resistance fighters who accept that their mission is unlikely to produce any benefits may still feel that 'something has to be done' to make a protest. The motive here is what Weber called an 'ethic of conviction', as distinct from an 'ethic of responsibility' that modifies goals according to what is realistically achievable. (Margaret Thatcher was proud to describe herself as a 'conviction politician' and unlike her 'wet' predecessors.)

These types of action can be combined. Traditions can be invented; rituals copied. Politicians can appear to rage at one another and then be seen drinking together happily after the debate. There is, Weber believed, an underlying process of rationalisation in modernity, expressed in different ways in the systematisation of administrative processes, legal codes, business practices and even religions. Weber is known as the great theorist of bureaucracy. Any type of administration, he argued, will tend to become more formalised. Formal systems may not be more efficient, but they are more reliable and 'technically superior'; once established, they tend not to be abolished unless the whole organisation collapses. However, people may develop informal strategies to get round the formal rules: use of personal contacts, telephone calls rather than written communications and so on.

Weber's concept of bureaucracy is a neutral one, but he recognises its pathological dimension, in which the operation of the 'machine' becomes an end in itself. (One of the best episodes of the television comedy *Yes, Minister* features a hospital with no patients, where the administration works perfectly.) In politics, Weber was particularly concerned about 'rule by officials' and the bureaucratisation of career politicians, pinning his hopes on a directly elected president who could cut through the red tape and give genuine political direction. He also wanted Germany to have a stronger parliament, not so much for democratic reasons as to train a more capable political class.

Weber described himself as a 'class-conscious bour-geois': his politics were liberal and strongly nationalist. He believed, however, in a sharp separation between the practice of social science and the expression of political or other values. This was partly to avoid the contamination of science by value judgements (the aspect which became a commonplace in twentieth-century social science), but for Weber it was just as important to realise that values should be freely chosen rather than believed to be underwritten by social analysis. Be a Marxist, an anarchist, a pacifist or a nationalist if you want to, says Weber, but don't kid yourself that your commitment follows logically from your social science. This, along with his early death, is part of the expla-nation for the fact that there was no 'Weberian School' or paradigm in the sense of the followers of Marx or Durk-heim, but his more diffuse influence has been as strong in social theory as Durkheim's.

More interesting perhaps for the history of social theory is the way subsequent thinkers have brought together Marx and Weber. The most important contribution is that by the Hungarian Marxist Georg Lukács, who had attended Simmel's lectures in Berlin and was a regular guest at the Webers' in Heidelberg. Lukács brought together Marx's idea of the 'fetishism' of commodities with Weber's concept of rationalisation in what he called 'reification' – the transfor-mation of social relations between people into things. What for Marx is an inevitably exploitative and essentially antag-onistic social relation between worker and employer is transformed into 'the rate for the job'. The underlying idea that human products come, like Frankenstein, to dominate and threaten their producers was not new, but the term 'reification', which Lukács took from Simmel, was such a natural development of Marx's thought that it is often thought to be one of his core concepts. (The word appears only once in Marx's *Capital*.)

Reification is central to neo-Marxist critical theory, especially the thought of Theodor Adorno. Adorno, along with Max Horkheimer, was the key figure in the critical theory of the Frankfurt School, linked to the Institute of Social Research based in Frankfurt and, for a time, in exile in New York. Adorno and Horkheimer's *Dialectic of Enlightenment* (1947) included a critique of mass culture, or what they called the 'culture industry'. In Adorno's pessimistic vision, 'What philosophy once called life has turned into the sphere of the private and then merely of consumption.' Capitalist exploitation is just one aspect of domination. The result is what another thinker associated with the Frankfurt School, Herbert Marcuse, called 'one-dimensional' or uncritical thought in his influential 1964 book, *One-Dimensional Man*.

In making domination central to his analysis, Adorno was in a sense following Max Weber, whose Nietzschean emphasis on power complements Marx's focus on exploitation. Weber, who once said that the seriousness of a thinker could be measured by their response to Marx and Nietzsche, broadened Marx's focus on class by analysing classes, status groups (such as the 'estates' of feudal societies) and political parties as aspects of the distribution of *power*. In the late twentieth century, Theda Skocpol in the US and a cluster of British sociologists (Anthony Giddens, Michael Mann and Martin Shaw) picked up the themes of state power, interstate relations, nationalism and war, bridging the gap between sociology and the relatively new field of international relations, with its roots in the history of diplomacy and warfare (see Chapter 7).

Whereas Marx offered the prospect of a society in which exploitation and alienation were abolished by communism, the Frankfurt theorists were responding to the failure of the working class to support communism in the West, the degeneration of the Russian Revolution into dictatorship and the triumph of fascism in much of Europe. Even the defeat of fascism and Nazism in 1945 did not promise much hope that modern societies could overcome the situation Marcuse described in the opening sentence of *One-Dimensional Man*: 'A comfortable, smooth, reasonable, democratic unfreedom prevails in advanced industrial civilization, a token of technical progress.'

The term 'reification' is taken up in what is sometimes called a second (post-war) generation of critical theory by Jürgen Habermas in his account of capitalism in *The Theory of Communicative Action* (1981) and, in a third generation, by Axel Honneth. It is used in a different way by Peter Berger and Thomas Luckmann in their *Social Construction of Reality* (1966), which gave rise to the 'social constructionist' approach discussed in the next chapter. Here it refers to the way in which we take for granted social phenomena that are largely the product of our own acts of definition. (Stereotypes of gender or ethnicity are a good example.)

Habermas, in his 'reconstruction' of historical materialism and his own 'theory of communicative action', gives as much prominence to Weber as to Marx. He uses a theory of action that builds on but goes beyond Weber in order to rework the Marxist critique of capitalism. Brilliantly spanning the theories discussed in previous chapters of this book and in the coming chapter, he argues for a model of communicative action that underlies existing theories of action.

Habermas discusses three standard models of action. One of these is Weber's model of purposive-rational action, which Habermas calls 'strategic': manipulating people as you manipulate other aspects of your environment in order to achieve a given end. The second is what he calls normatively regulated action: the functionalist idea that people's action and role behaviour are governed by their respect for a shared system of values. Third is the dramaturgical model of action, explored in the next chapter, which stresses the idea of social action as a performance. All three of these partial approaches, Habermas argues, rely on a more fundamental idea of communicative action in which people aim to come to an agreement about states of affairs in the outside world, about their internal feelings and emotional states, about what is morally right and legitimate, and what should be done.

The example Habermas gives is of a professor asking one of the students in a seminar to fetch him a glass of water. They're not in the army, so this is a request, not an order, and the recipient can question it along these lines. First, the factual assumption that there is an available water source in the building. Second, whether the professor really wants a glass of water or is just trying to show up one of his students in front of the others. Third, whether he has the right to ask this: the student may reply, for example, 'I'm not your servant.'

We seem to have come a long way from the analysis of modernity and capitalism, but Habermas uses this model of action to show how, in European modernity from around the seventeenth century, people came to question traditional beliefs and authorities and to think about the rational reordering of social relations. In the French Revolution at the end of the eighteenth century, for example, Reason was put in the place of the Christian and other gods. What then happens, Habermas argues, is that this process of rationalisation is overlaid by a second one which again *removes* areas of social life from rational discussion, as economic and administrative systems take on a life of their own. As we now tend to say, 'The computer says no': the formal system of credit or law refuses to admit of argument. Your credit account is up to its limit, your welfare claim doesn't fit the criteria, and that's that. Habermas's version of the Marxist critique of capitalism is to suggest that we might have had the first of these rationalisation processes, the criticism of tradition and the rise of independent argument, without the second: the uncoupling of formal economic and administrative processes from exposure to discussion and agreement. Less speculatively, he criticises the tendency of these systems to 'colonise' more informal areas of social life, as more and more areas become marketised and regulated: for example, surrogate parenting or the sale of body parts. The prenuptial contract may cast a shadow over the impending marriage.

Here, then, is one way in which social action at the most basic level links up with broader processes of social and historical development and with the idea of evolutionary learning mentioned earlier.

5

HOW IS SOCIETY POSSIBLE?

Here is a classic philosophical question, given a sociological answer: the eighteenth-century philosopher Imma-
nuel Kant had asked how a pure science of nature (such as
Newtonian mechanics) is *possible*; his answer was that we
sort our experience of the world according to categories of
space, time, causality and so on. As we saw in Chapter 3,
Durkheim's sociology of knowledge was based on the social
shaping of these categories (social space, social time, social
power). Weber's friend Georg Simmel suggested more radically that human society is based essentially on our awareness of being part of a society. Whereas we human observ-
ers order the natural world according to our perspectives
on it (the perspectives of medium-sized animals standing
upright), Simmel argued that 'the unity of society needs
no observer'. Society is based, in short, on our ideas about
society and, most importantly, the idea that we form a
society made up of people like ourselves.

Simmel wrote just a few pages on his theme, as an 'excursus' or interlude in a much larger overview of the new discipline of sociology. His most substantial work, *The Philosophy of Money* (1900), could as easily have been called the
sociology or the psychology of money. Simmel examined
the intellectual, cultural and psychological preconditions
of the money economy and, most of all, its consequences.

He is also known for his shorter studies on the city and the two themes are intimately connected. Cities rely on money: they need to import most of their food from outside. People move into, out of and around cities by paying to travel on mass transit systems. Cities are also the centre of finance; Marx had earlier compared the old gods of Mount Olympus with the new superhuman powers of banks and insurance companies. And social relations in cities, much more than in rural communities, are relations between strangers, often mediated by money.

All this, said Simmel, means that the money economy and city life are dominated by a rationalistic, calculating attitude. Time is part of this. You no longer walk to work in the fields when it gets light; you hurry to catch the 8.30 train so as to be in the office by 9. (Some early films known as 'city symphonies' are typically structured around the clock-time of a day in the city.) Marx loved Shakespeare and often quoted him in his critique of money and capital. Simmel was more ambivalent (about capitalism, not Shakespeare). For Simmel, city life and a money economy encourage individualism and a form of freedom; on the other hand, they generate nervousness (this was a major theme of the late nineteenth and early twentieth centuries and one of the sources of Sigmund Freud's work). This nervousness, resulting from crowds, noise, bustle and so on, in cities is compensated for, according to Simmel, by a 'blasé' attitude and an avoidance of contact with other people. (Is the person lying on the pavement sleeping or dying? Better not stop and get involved.) Unlike Weber, Simmel did not make a fuss about 'value-free' social science, but he shared Weber's view that the role of the sociologist is not to praise or blame, but to understand.

Simmel wrote big books, but his great strength is as an essayist, jumping from one topic to another in an approach that has been called sociological impressionism. His attention to culture (including fashion) makes him seem in many ways the most modern of the classical social theorists. Translate his slightly old-fashioned writing style into modern English and he could pass for a twenty-first-century professor of cultural studies. His idea of society as the product of human acts of definition is an early expression of one of the main currents of social theory, often called social constructionism, which is the subject of this chapter.

When Simmel asked how society is possible he was thinking in very general terms, in which our sense of being part of a society actually makes up the content of that society. The same idea, in a more concrete form, can be found, for example, in Benedict Anderson's influential conception of nationalism as 'imagined communities'. In Anderson's analysis, in a book with that title published in 1983, we don't of course know most of our fellow citizens (even if we are Luxembourgers, let alone Germans or Americans), but nationalism as an ideology, and the national state as the 'default mode' of modern politics, tell us that we have something in common with them. 'Three Britons dead in jumbo jet disaster' reads the UK newspaper headline, with equivalents in other countries. 'Print capitalism' – books and papers in the 'national' language – is in fact an important mechanism in Anderson's explanation of the rise of national consciousness.

More broadly, Simmel's answer to his question is at the origin of the 'social construction of reality' or social constructionism in social theory. His approach was also taken up in the mid-twentieth century in the 'phenomenological' sociology of the Austrian-American Alfred Schütz, in Erving Goffman's analyses of 'the presentation of self in everyday life' in a book with that title and in the 'ethnomethodology' of another North American, Harold Garfinkel. Schütz asked, in a sense, how Max Weber's interpretive sociology was possible. Whereas Weber had moved rather quickly to the classification of action according to his four types, Schütz concentrated on the prior processes of typification in everyday life. I see a uniformed figure through the frosted glass of my front door. Is it the postman, or the meter reader, or a police officer, or someone impersonating one of them? We have what Schütz called a 'stock of knowledge at hand', knowledge which is 'taken for granted' and which we bring to bear in such situations. As Schütz put it, 'The constructs used by the social scientist are, so to speak, constructs of the second degree, namely constructs of the constructs made by the actors on the social scene.'

Schütz describes our knowledge of others in terms of concentric circles or 'worlds'. There is the world of our immediate friends and family, whom we know well, the world of people we have met at one time or another (estimates put this figure at around 5,000 in a lifetime) and the world of people we know *about* but do not know personally. He is interested, then, in the way in which the social world appears or is 'given' to us.

Simmel wrote a lot about the aesthetic dimension of social life, with essays on fashion and other aspects of self-presentation. The way we ourselves appear to others is also the focus of Erving Goffman's work. Note the term 'actor' in the quote above from Schütz. It can simply mean someone performing an action, which is all Schütz probably meant there, or it can mean someone playing a part. Goffman stressed the theatrical or performance aspect of our every-day lives. Houses typically have a division between 'front-stage' rooms, where visitors are received, and more private areas. We probably dress differently from usual for a job interview, and present ourselves differently than in more informal situations. In his later work Goffman stressed the idea of 'framing', which has been very influential in cultural and media studies as well as in sociology. An interview may take the form of a conversation, and may even be conducted over a meal, but it is framed in a different way. Joking typically plays on the interface between frames; someone who 'can't take a joke' may have rejected a shift of frame. Politics, too, can be reframed, as when heckling makes a speaker look ridiculous. A turning point at the beginning of the Romanian revolution of 1989 occurred when the audience bussed in to hear and applaud a speech by the dictator switched from cheering to jeering. (Unable to frame this in an acceptable way, the TV simply stopped transmission.)

Goffman's stress on the performance dimension of acting out social roles illustrates the way in which a social constructionist approach allows us to rethink a central category of social theory. The idea of a social role has a long history: Shakespeare wrote that 'one man in his time plays many parts'. Functionalist sociology tends to take roles very seriously, rather as a British Hegelian philosopher wrote of 'my station and its duties'. In the functionalist model we are socialised into roles prescribed by society, with 'role distance', a half-hearted or ironic role performance, as when a prime minister says 'I'm an ordinary sort of guy', being the exception rather than the rule. Goffman's image, like that of interactionist sociology more generally, tends to be closer to theatrical improvisation, with one aspect of role distance at least displayed by actors 'hamming it up'. Among the more readable passages in the existentialist philosopher Jean-Paul Sartre's *Being and Nothingness* (1943) is a description of a café waiter *playing* his role with exaggerated gestures, sending up the waiter role.

If Goffman's approach to role performance seems more convincing today than the functionalist approach, it is perhaps because of the increased informality of many aspects of contemporary life (though there is also a counter-trend to formalise job descriptions, performance indicators and so on). A nice example of an interactionist approach to the medical role is provided by Howard Becker and his co-authors in *Boys in White* (1963); the title itself demystifies the status of the trainee doctor. Gendered behaviour can also be plausibly analysed as performance, as in the influential work of the US philosopher and cultural theorist Judith Butler.

Ethnography, the careful observation and description of social situations, is an approach common to Simmel and the constructionist tradition. Goffman began his work with ethnographic field research in the Shetland Islands;

Harold Garfinkel, who had studied with the functionalist system theorist Talcott Parsons, began by analysing the way US jurors engage in 'practical reasoning' to make a judgement about the guilt or innocence of the accused. He called this approach 'ethnomethodology', on the analogy of the anthropological specialisms of ethnobotany, ethnomusicology and so on. In Garfinkel's approach, the maintenance of order is not the product of collective values, as in Durkheim's or Parsons's sociology, but a more fragile accomplishment of social actors' interpretive work. His so-called 'breaching' experiments demonstrated this by disrupting or breaching our taken-for-granted routines of greeting and so on. When people say 'How are you?' they don't expect a detailed description of your physical and mental state of the kind you might give to a doctor. Try it, said Garfinkel, and then try to pick up the pieces. In another of his experiments, researchers posed as counsellors and gave a random sequence of yes/no answers to questions; the bewildered clients tried to make sense of these. One of the chapters in Garfinkel's *Studies in Ethnomethodology* (1967) is about a transsexual person, Agnes, learning and reflecting as an adult on norms and habits of feminine behaviour which, if she had begun as a woman, she would have presumably learned more informally. Role performance and regular social practices such as turn-taking in conversation involve an informal script of rules which frame behaviour in desired ways. If you telephone someone, for example, it should probably be you, rather than the person who takes the call, who ends the conversation with some polite formula.

The detailed analysis of conversation has become an important element of sociolinguistics. Although sometimes seen as too relativistic and even frivolous, elements of the work of Goffman and Garfinkel were taken up and modified in more structural approaches such as those of Pierre Bourdieu and Anthony Giddens. Bourdieu's key notion of what he called the habitus, a way of behaving in language (including body language), consumption practices and so on which is shaped by, expresses and reproduces inequalities of class and power, owes much to Goffman's model of self-presentation. Bourdieu also extended the notion of capital to 'cultural capital', embodied in educational credentials and in more diffuse capacities such as the ability to use complex language or to speak knowledgeably about fine wines, atonal music or other phenomena associated with 'distinction' (the title of one of his major books).

Giddens followed Garfinkel in stressing the 'knowledgeability' of social actors: the idea that in order to be a functioning member of a human society you have to have a quite developed informal sociological understanding of how societies work. Children learn at an early age to ask for sweets from the parent or carer most likely to succumb to pestering, but also not to accept them from strangers. We know that it's polite to greet strangers in the country but peculiar to do so in a town. In a polarised society such as Northern Ireland, people often claim they can 'tell' whether strangers in the street are Catholics or Protestants, based on accent, appearance and other cues, such as the route of a bus they may have disembarked from. Again, Simmel's emphasis on style and Schütz's notion of typification can be seen to play a part in the informal maintenance of order in social life.

The links which Simmel so brilliantly described between everyday behaviour and interpretation and larger structural processes are also central to the work of the great historical sociologist Norbert Elias. Elias's major work, *On the Process of Civilisation* (1939), moved from an analysis of etiquette manuals in early modern Europe to a study of the formation of the modern state. The respect for personal space expressed in table manners or injunctions not to fart, spit or urinate in the presence of others has analogies at the state level in the way states established order, monopolised the means of violence by eliminating private armies, monitored their borders and so on. Max Weber had described such processes in terms of a shift to legal-rational or bureaucratic rule and his overall conception of rationalisation, but Elias gave these ideas a further important twist.

Another key theorist in the second half of the twentieth century, Michel Foucault, also spanned these different dimensions of social analysis. Foucault's first work was on 'madness' in the eighteenth century, the 'age of reason'. Why, he asked, did people start to construct madness as a medical problem and, more particularly, start locking 'mad' people up in asylums? He ingeniously suggested that with the elimination of leprosy in Europe the secluded leper hospitals were ripe for reuse. Thus began one of Foucault's main areas of research, on prisons, hospitals and more generally the government of bodies, which intersected with the other main strand of his work, on the history of ideas and academic disciplines. Like madness, homosexuality was reconceptualised in the nineteenth century as a lasting identity rather than a term to describe behaviour: 'the homosexual' was stereotyped, medicalised and often treated.

The medical look or 'gaze' was another key theme for Foucault: the examination of patients with a view to diagnosis. This might include hospitalisation, where, as in prisons, inmates were subject to surveillance, 'under observation'. Foucault made much of the utilitarian philosopher Jeremy Bentham's 'panopticon' design in 1791 for a prison where inmates in their cells could be observed from a central control point. Once the possibility of permanent observation was established, the observation point did not even have to be manned; inmates would monitor their own conduct just in case they were being observed. (An important film made in 2006, *The Lives of Others*, portrays the effects of the surveillance system in communist East Germany.)

Social and political theory, Foucault suggested, had paid too much attention to formal politics and issues of sovereignty, and not enough to more fundamental processes of the governing and disciplining of populations. His book on punishment and surveillance, *Discipline and Punish* (1975), contrasts the exemplary public execution of someone who had tried to kill Louis XV with the regular, sustained and ordered punishment regime of the modern prison. Foucault's ideas were very influential in social policy, with 'decarceration' of mental patients becoming an established practice in Italy and elsewhere. His stress on surveillance has been seen to be particularly relevant to modern 'audit societies', in which everything must be monitored, however pointlessly.

Anthony Giddens followed Foucault in making surveillance one of the 'institutional dimensions of modernity', along with industrialism, capitalism and military power. Industrialism and capitalism are long-standing categories of sociological analysis, but there are fewer sociological studies of militarism and warfare, which tend to be found in the related discipline known as international relations. Although the notion of surveillance (and self-surveillance) has echoes of Max Weber's analysis of self-control in his essays on the Protestant Ethic and of Norbert Elias's concept of 'affect control', it was Foucault, with his image of the pan-optical prison, who put it on the map.

In his later work, from the mid-1970s to his death in 1984, Foucault moved from an emphasis on power and domination which recalls Weber and Adorno to a focus on 'self-fashioning' in sexuality and other areas of everyday life. In particular, he turned back to Greek thought for what he seems to have seen as a healthier attitude to life than that presented in the rather humourless and moralising religions emanating from the Middle East: Judaism, Christianity and Islam. Modern sexual morality was finally emerging from this focus on what Christianity called 'the world, the flesh and the devil'.

This aspect of Foucault's work and the notion of an ethics of the body and the self, as well as his earlier focus on disciplinary power, have been taken up in important ways in feminist theory. A major slogan of the 'second-wave feminism' of the later twentieth century was that 'the personal is political'; Foucault was in a sense arguing that the political is, among other things, personal (and bodily). The fact that much gender politics involves couples and families, sexuality and male violence against women, means that, although Foucault did not particularly focus on gender, the relevance of his work is undeniable – perhaps more than that of Bourdieu, who explicitly addressed the topic of male domination in a book with that title in 1998.

Foucault's turn back to Greek history and the concept of self-knowledge was also a way for him to get at the basic structures of consciousness in modernity: something that had shaped his earlier work on madness and also on the history of ideas in *The Order of Things* (1966). The central theme in both areas of investigation is the reduction of truth to a matter of knowledge by human subjects: the 'Cartesian moment' when Descartes, in 1637, grounded his knowledge in his certainty of his own existence as a thinking being ('I think, therefore I am.'). It is only much later, with the philosophy of the nineteenth century and in Marxism and psychoanalysis, that we find a return to a more social conception of the subject of knowledge and the conditions of knowledge. Foucault's own work is of course a further example of this. He provides in a sense two histories of social theory or the human sciences: one more theoretical, focused on the concept of 'man' and frameworks of thought which he called *épistèmes* and which parallel Kuhn's paradigms; and the other more materialist, on the way in which forms of knowledge interact and reflect social order and discipline.

Here, though neither of them seems to have registered it, at least in print, is an important area of convergence between Foucault and Bourdieu. From his early work on the 'craft' of sociology to his posthumously published 'self-analysis' in 2004 (though he had used the term 'self-analysis' as early as 1984), Bourdieu constantly stressed the idea of reflexivity, that all work in sociology and the other social sciences needed to be preceded by a process of reflection on the researcher's own social position and the ways in which this might influence the study: a 'sociology of knowledge' practised by the sociologist on him or herself. His work on class and education addressed issues of the relation between knowledge, class position and power (or, as he tended to call it, symbolic violence) which resonate strongly with Foucault's work. Systems of classification, such as those which produced the rank order in the *aggrégation* exam which both of them took (Bourdieu only a few years after Foucault), 'classify the classifiers'. Both Bourdieu and Foucault, despite the privileged positions they attained in French intellectual life, had suffered from social discrimination: class prejudice in Bourdieu's case (he came from humble origins in a remote part of south-west France), homophobia for Foucault. The work of both of them had an important autobiographical dimension: Foucault often said that his books could be read as 'autobiographical fragments' and Bourdieu addressed this topic more directly in his 'socio-analysis of himself'.

One of the most direct links to Simmel can be found in the classic book by Peter Berger and Thomas Luckmann, *The Social Construction of Reality* (1966). 'Everyday knowledge', they pointed out, does not just reflect but creates social reality. Think of two people who 'get together'; they will rapidly start to refer to themselves as 'we', and to form joint habits added to, or perhaps replacing, those they had before. Even on a short holiday or in the first days in a new house, people learn 'how to do things' and this knowledge becomes an automatic or 'taken-for-granted' feature. The idea of social construction has been prominent in postmodern theory, as well as in the US philosopher John Searle's analysis of money in *The Construction of Social Reality* (1995). A banknote is just a piece of paper or, in more recent forms, plastic; it is social definition that gives it value.

The more extreme versions of postmodern theory, such as Jean Baudrillard's announcement in 1982 of the 'End of the Social', his rejection of the distinction between the real and the 'simulacrum' or his claim that the (first) Gulf War did not take place (he was in fact jokingly referring to the title of a play about the Trojan War , while also intending to bring out the way in which the Gulf War was turned into a spectacle), have drifted out of fashion. What remains is a sense of the fragmentation or, in the Polish British sociologist Zygmunt Bauman's image, 'liquidity' of many aspects of contemporary reality. Theorists such as Luc Boltanski, who had earlier worked with Bourdieu, stress the 'fragility' of social reality, that 'institutions are without foundation'. Boltanski takes 'seriously the constant unease about what is and what is valid, which . . . is forcefully expressed in moments of dispute'. This contrasts with much twentieth-century thought, which had focused instead on the crushing force of large-scale structures of class and power.

We are still living with these tensions: sometimes the world seems impossible to change; at other moments we are confronted by the alternative image of radically different possibilities, exciting or (more often) threatening. In this sense, perhaps, the spectre of postmodernity still haunts us. Our image of the real has undoubtedly changed. What is more real: the value of an internet company with hardly any human workers or physical sites, or an obsolete and worthless rust-belt factory that once employed thousands of workers and supplied vital components across the world? A book may be marketed for $100 or more, or pirated and downloaded for nothing. The same plane journey may cost nothing but the price of the taxes, or hundreds of dollars.

Interpretive social theory, as pioneered by Simmel and Weber, raises big questions about social theory as a whole. I address these in more detail in the final chapter of this book, but it should already be clear that interpretive theory is not just one variant but a necessary accompaniment to all social theorising. Society, I would argue, is not 'all in the mind', but it is, in part, in our minds as well as in our spatial and other social relations. Even Durkheim, who wasn't keen on referring to internal mental processes, couldn't avoid referring constantly to his informal knowledge of 'what it's like' to be in a social situation of a particular type. This tacit knowledge of social life 'from the inside' is a crucial resource, not an impediment. Social theory is inevitably located, as the German sociologist Wolf Lepenies put it in the subtitle of a book of 1985, *Between Literature and Science* (also used as the title of the English edition).

A 'Simmelian School' of social theory is hardly conceivable, but phenomenological sociology, interactionism and ethnomethodology are recognisably distinct approaches and in this limited sense paradigms, and the idea of social construction, now often associated with postmodernism but actually with fairly clear starting points in Simmel's 'excursus' and then in Berger and Luckmann's classic book, can reasonably be seen as a paradigmatic innovation.

6

DISCOVERING THE UNCONSCIOUS

Sigmund Freud would probably have been the first to admit that his ventures into what we normally think of as social theory are not the strongest elements of his work. What is more important, however, is the fact that his analysis of the psyche has fundamentally shaped our understanding of humanity and hence of culture and society. This chapter will outline Freud's work in this area and trace its implications through to the present.

The term 'unconscious' and the idea of mental processes of which we are not aware had been knocking around from the beginning of the nineteenth century, but it was towards the end of the century that Freud began to develop what one of his mentor and collaborator Joseph Breuer's patients called a 'talking cure'. The patient, Bertha Pappenheim, to whom Breuer and Freud gave the pseudonym Anna O. when they wrote up the treatment in 1895, was suffering from headaches, disturbed vision, episodes of paralysis, an inability to speak her native language and other disorders which we would now call psychosomatic. Under hypnosis, Breuer encouraged her to revisit painful episodes in her life and her description of them seemed to relieve the symptoms. She was able, for example, to trace back her inability to drink water to her disgust at seeing a dog drinking out of a water glass, and remembering this episode enabled her to drink again. Was she putting some of this on because she was attracted to Breuer and appreciated his attention? Freud thought so, and this relationship of transference between patient and analyst became an important part of his understanding of his own practice. (The sexual politics of psychoanalysis is certainly dubious, as the feminist critics discussed later have pointed out.)

Whatever the truth about this early case, psychoanalysis was launched as a treatment and a theory, and in 1900 Freud published a major work on dreams, which he later called the 'royal route' to the discovery of the unconscious activities of the mind. He had earlier written to his collaborator Wilhelm Fliess:

> Do you suppose that some day a marble tablet will be placed on the house, inscribed with these words:
> In This House, on July 24th, 1895
> the Secret of Dreams was Revealed
> to Dr. Sigm. Freud.

Freud certainly fancied the idea of himself as a discoverer; in an earlier letter to Fliess he wrote that he was not so much a scientist as 'by temperament nothing but a *conquistador*'. Freud's theory of dreams is centred on the idea of wish-fulfilment: we can dream of doing things we wouldn't allow ourselves to think about when conscious. Most prominent among these unconscious wishes is the alleged desire of male infants to kill their fathers and marry their mothers: what Freud called the Oedipus complex.

Much of Freud's dream analysis also involves complicated wordplay in a variety of languages, and 'slips of the tongue' (or of the pen) are another expression, he thought, of unconscious or repressed wishes. 'Pleased to eat you,' says the executive to the victim of an impending takeover bid. Or, in one of Freud's own examples from his *Psychopathology of Everyday Life* (1901), a bossy woman says of her husband, who has been told by the doctor that he does not need to obey any dietary restrictions, 'He can eat whatever I want.'

Where do we go with all this? What relevance does a therapeutic practice (which may or may not be effective) have for social theory? We might start by asking what role neurosis and psychopathology play in social life. Many political leaders are deeply disturbed; at least one of Mrs Thatcher's ministers resigned because he thought she was going off the rails. Research over the past ten years or so has explored the place of the psychopath in modern business. One of the key texts was titled *Snakes in Suits* (2006); the authors, Paul Babiak and Robert Hare, said they were less concerned about executives who were overtly aggressive 'than about those who are willing to use their "deadly charm" to con and manipulate others'.

But this is just the tip of a big iceberg. Take the concept of authority. We've looked at this in the work of Marx, Weber and Durkheim, but we learn about authority as infants and our childhood experiences and unconscious impulses may, as Freud believed, shape our adult behaviour. When does a 'healthy respect for authority' become conformism or a craving for a father figure? I'm authoritative; you're bossy; s/he's authoritarian.

Freud and the physicist Albert Einstein corresponded at

the beginning of the 1930s in an exchange published under the title 'Why War?' There Freud repeated the analysis he had given in 1930 in a short book known in English as *Civilization and Its Discontents*. Human culture is built in part on the repression of conscious and unconscious drives. This process is necessary: the ego, referring to the superego or conscience, has to control impulses arising from the id. In Freud's slogan: 'Where the id was, the ego should be.' Repression, however, also has a psychic cost. Catholic priests, for example, forbidden to have sex with other people in socially acceptable forms, have been known to molest their parishioners. As with the unconscious, the theme of repression is not a new one: William Blake wrote, 'He who desires, but acts not, breeds pestilence.' Freud, though, gave it a more cautious and formal treatment.

Freud's *Mass Psychology and Ego Analysis* (often mistranslated as 'group psychology'), which he wrote in 1921, addresses the classic theme of the relation between the individual and social forms, distinguishing here between 'primary' masses, such as tribes and crowds, and 'artificial' masses, such as armies and churches with a formal structure. He also wrote about religion in *Moses and Monotheism* (1939) and in two earlier books, *Totem and Taboo* (1912–13) and one whose title conveys the essential message, *The Future of an Illusion* (1927).

We can also see Freud, like Simmel, writing about, and out of, the experience of modernity, with all its novel and fragmented impressions brought together, for example, in dreams, but in jokes as well, which typically juxtapose contradictory frames of reference. Like dreams, our waking life also brings together past and present; we may 'act out' or repeat childhood experiences or actions, or repeat habits formed in childhood, in our adult professional and private lives. Freud's ideas can also be linked to those of Marx, whose account of 'commodity fetishism' in capitalism draws on contemporary anthropology too. Both can be seen as realists in the sense of modern critical realist philosophy: looking below surface appearances, such as the wage contract or bourgeois moral conduct, to deeper underlying structures of exploitation (for Marx) or fantasy and underlying impulses and their repression (for Freud).

There are also parallels with Weber and Durkheim. The idea of obsessive work and self-mastery which Weber described in *The Protestant Ethic and the Spirit of Capitalism* is something which preoccupied Freud as well (and both were what we would now call workaholics). Weber's model of authority, especially charismatic authority, has parallels with Freud's: charismatic rulers often address unconscious feelings among their followers. Finally, Freud's stress on regulation recalls Durkheim's anxieties about what he called anomie or normlessness in modern societies.

The twentieth century saw a number of people attempt to bring together Marx and Freud. The most prominent among these was Wilhelm Reich, who worked in Freud's clinic in Vienna before moving to Berlin, then Oslo and finally emigrating to the US, where he died in 1957. His work on character influenced the analyst Anna Freud, Freud's daughter, and his idea of the armoured body was taken up much later by Klaus Theweleit in his analysis of the *Freikorps* paramilitaries in Germany who prefigured

Nazism, *Male Fantasies* (1977). Reich himself analysed *The Mass Psychology of Fascism* (1933). His enthusiastic support of sexual liberation was controversial; his promotion of boxes to accumulate what he called orgone energy, though these were well received by a number of celebrities, including Norman Mailer and Sean Connery, led to a prison sentence during which he died. The Yugoslav director Dušan Makavejev made a film about him in 1971, *W.R.: Mysteries of the Organism.*

Less dramatically, Erich Fromm and Herbert Marcuse, both associated with the Frankfurt Institute for Social Research, also brought together socialist and psychoanalytic ideas. Marcuse's *Eros and Civilization* (1955) argued that over and above the instinctual repression necessary for civilisation there was a 'surplus repression' in capitalist societies which restricted human possibilities for liberation – an idea which he developed further in his very influential book of 1964, *One-Dimensional Man*. Theodor Adorno, the Institute's most important thinker, combined a more orthodox approach to Freudian theory with the Marxism he also applied to the analysis of society and culture, including his analysis of authoritarianism discussed in the next chapter. In Adorno's work, as in that of the others, Freudian theory is used to explain the accommodation of individuals to capitalism and, more fundamentally, the whole question of the relationship between the individual and society.

Jürgen Habermas, who is usually seen as the main representative of a second generation of Frankfurt School critical theory, in his work of the mid-1960s also pointed to the methodological parallels between Marxism and psychoanalysis. The Marxist critique of economic theory aims not only to show its errors but to expose the reasons why it is accepted and why it appears plausible, just as psychoanalysis can help us to understand our irrational fears (for example, the fear of spiders in a country like the UK where the local species are harmless), and behaviour which may disturb ourselves and/or others. Both Marxism and psychoanalysis go beyond the *interpretation* of ideologies or problematic behaviour to identify causal obstacles to understanding. Someone who tries to understand an ideology like Nazism will also want to ask *why* people adopted such an irrational view of the world, just as, if I start to speak or behave oddly, you may at some point stop arguing with me and suggest I get professional help.

Also in the 1960s, the French Marxist philosopher Louis Althusser used the psychoanalytic concept of 'overdetermination', in which dreams are produced both by recent memories and past traumas and by unconscious drives, in his reformulation of Marx's account of the relationship between the productive 'base' and the legal-political 'superstructure'. The economic level, Althusser argued, is primary or determinant 'only in the last instance': at times of rapid social change, such as the Russian Revolution of 1917, the political level may be dominant. So, as Lenin and the Bolsheviks argued, they didn't need to wait for capitalism to develop further in Russia in order to have a communist revolution. Althusser also used psychoanalytic theory, as developed by his contemporary Jacques Lacan, in his analysis of ideology. This should be seen, he argued, not as a false or distorted reflection of reality, as in Marx's model of the upside-down image in the camera obscura, but as a lived relation to reality – imaginary not in the sense of non-existent or made up but as involving the imagination. Like Durkheim, Althusser stressed the need for a break with this common-sense relation to the world in the development of systematic social theory. Despite their very different political orientations (liberal in Durkheim's case and Marxist in Althusser's), they shared a suspicion of common sense, where other theorists, such as Weber and Simmel, saw social science as building on common-sense understanding.

The former position of course raises the stakes for social theory if it claims a scientific status. Both Marx and Freud saw themselves as scientists, but the theories of each of them have been hotly disputed between enthusiastic and even dogmatic followers and people who take a radically sceptical view of one or both theories. In the case of psychoanalytic theory, Lacan, like Althusser, was strongly influenced by structural linguistics, and he argued that the unconscious was 'structured like a language'. More sceptically, Sebastiano Timpanaro suggested that 'slips of the tongue' could just as easily be explained by purely linguistic processes: no need to wheel out the unconscious. Drawing on his expertise in textual criticism, Timpanaro argued that most mistakes in transcription are simply 'errors due to distraction'. This was part of a broader critique by Timpanaro of Freud's style of argumentation and general approach, shared by critics who objected to other aspects, such as the 'untestability' of the theory and the likelihood that the good done by the 'talking cure', if any, was more likely to be because of the fact of talking, rather than the theory or any interpretation provided.

Medical patients often feel better after a conversation with the doctor, even if s/he has given them no treatment or just a placebo. The Czech British anthropologist and philosopher Ernest Gellner, who was utterly sceptical about psychoanalytic theory, accepted that transference, the attachment of the patient to the analyst, was an important mechanism and that psychoanalysis was right to stress 'the importance of instinctual drives, and of the complexity and deviousness of the semantic forms in which they appear in consciousness'. Here again we can see the ways in which we may not want to adopt a social theory wholesale, while recognising the role it has played in contemporary culture and drawing on its partial view of the world to develop our own understanding. If I wrote a book about capitalism without mentioning Marx, or about psychopathology without mentioning Freud, you would wonder why.

As we saw in the last chapter, Foucault began his career writing about madness, so an obvious question to ask is what he thought about psychoanalytic theory. The question is less easy to answer. He said he was thoroughly bored by his own analysis, though he was sympathetic to the emphasis on language in psychoanalytic theory and practice. In practical terms, he welcomed the fact that psychoanalysis was an alternative to a psychiatry based around asylums and that it introduced a new type of relationship between patient and analyst. But psychoanalysis, avoiding the treatment of anything diagnosed as psychosis, as opposed to neurosis, did not address much of the domain of psychiatry, and it was not in the end a fundamental challenge to the medical model.

Lacan's development of Freudian theory has been a major resource for another contemporary philosopher and social theorist, Slavoj Žižek. As with the attempts in the mid-twentieth century to marry Freud and Marx, Žižek aimed to show how we identify with, or even love, the capitalist and patriarchal structures that oppress us. This approach complements Foucault's stress on micro-power in social relations: our complicity in disciplinary power structures which, he stressed, is often more important than formal political power.

I mentioned earlier the problematic gender politics of psychoanalytic theory: its masculinist assumptions and its suspicion of minority sexual practices, often seen as 'perversions'. As in the case of Marxism, some feminist critics argued that the theory could be tweaked into an acceptable shape, while others rejected it as irredeemably flawed. It should be said that several of the earlier analysts and psychoanalytic theorists were female, even if you count Freud's daughter Anna as a special case. What we would now call homophobic prejudice, the idea that homosexual men or women were not suited to a career in psychoanalysis, was more of a problem in Britain and North America, with their residues of puritanical attitudes, than in sophisticated cities like Vienna, Berlin or Paris.

More recently, many of the leading theorists and defenders of psychoanalysis have been women: for example, Juliet Mitchell and Jacqueline Rose in Britain, and Julia Kristeva in France. Mitchell argued that Freud had simply failed to break out of the dominant patriarchal culture of his time, and she followed earlier twentieth-century feminists in arguing that Freud's critique of *femininity* had a strong feminist potential. Femininity, in other words, can be understood in a broader sense as an ideology and way of behaving which, though primarily associated with women, can affect men as well and restricts the potential of human beings regardless of their sex.

Whatever you think of psychoanalysis as a theory or a practice, it has had a major impact on the study of culture, inspiring many readings of literary texts and, most strikingly, in the analysis of cinema. There are obvious similarities between dreams and films, with similar disturbances and juxtapositions of time, and the experience of a cinema performance is also comparable to a dream. The themes of voyeurism and desire are obviously relevant, as is, a bit more speculatively, the idea that films get through to the unconscious in a way that theatre or other art forms may not. Several psychoanalytic theorists have devoted particular attention to cinema, notably Hanns Sachs and, later, Gilles Deleuze and Slavoj Žižek.

Deleuze, Kristeva and Žižek can all be seen as marking out a second wave of interaction between psychoanalysis and other strands of social theory. Whereas the first wave was dominated by the interface with Marxism, in the work of Reich, Fromm, Marcuse and Adorno (and to some extent continued by Habermas), in this second wave Marxism is important only for Žižek, although one of Deleuze's major books, the two-volume work written with the psychoanalyst Félix Guattari, has the title *Capitalism and Schizophrenia*, and at the time of his death he was planning a book on 'the greatness of Marx'. There remains an important area of intersection between social and psychological theory to be developed. Many opportunities have been missed because social psychology, especially in the English-speaking countries, has tended to follow a rather narrow scientific model.

As with Marxism, the term 'orthodox' haunts Freudian theory. Freud was always conscious that he was producing controversial ideas and techniques in a largely hostile environment, and suspicious of divergent approaches which might weaken the psychoanalytic movement. Those who broke away could readily be located in the theory of Oedipal revolt against the father. Freudian theorists and practitioners can still be dismissive of more diffuse forms of psychotherapy. From our point of view, however, the diversity of the approaches inspired by psychoanalytic theory is what makes it such a rich current of contemporary culture.

7

SOCIAL THEORY AND POLITICS

It will have become clear through the previous chapters that the interactions between social theory and politics are particularly close. At its most general, a conception of society or the social can be seen as a way of resolving political problems that politics alone had failed to solve – both theoretically and in the development of programmes and movements of social democracy out of liberal democracy. Then there is the contrast between explicitly political approaches, such as Marxism, feminism, post-colonial theory and critical race theory, and the more value-free aspirations of Weber, Durkheim or Simmel.

Social theorists, of whom three (Werner Sombart, Robert Michels and Norbert Elias) are discussed in this chapter, have also offered important analyses of politics. First, in *Why is There No Socialism in the United States?* (1906), Werner Sombart ran through a number of possible answers to the question he had posed. The economic condition of workers was generally better than in Europe. ('On the reefs of roast beef and apple pie,' he wrote, 'socialistic utopias of every sort are sent to their doom.') There was no aristocracy (though, of course, in the South plantation owners had managed a version of it with the aid of slavery), and the more egalitarian attitudes which Tocqueville had already observed eighty years earlier meant that relations between classes were less distant and antagonistic. Finally, if this was not enough to reconcile Americans to capitalism in the developed parts of the country, they could move west and set up independently.

Sombart's analysis, like Frederick Jackson Turner's 'frontier thesis' of 1893, has remained a reference point for discussion of American 'exceptionalism'. More recent research has tended to stress the diversity of political traditions and the dangers of contrasting a homogeneous Europe to an equally stereotyped America. The ways in which social structures and cultures impact on politics are very diverse, and the role of history and tradition which Montesquieu stressed are very important: in France, for example, to be a monarchist is to be part of an eccentric political minority, whereas in Britain it is republicanism that is the controversial minority view.

Sombart's contemporary Robert Michels followed Max Weber in asking, in his book *Political Parties* (1911), why organisations, in particular social democratic parties like the German SPD, become increasingly oligarchical in their structure. In a democracy, Michels argued, parties have to organise to compete for votes, and 'who says organisation, says oligarchy'. 'Grass-roots' militants become an embarrassment to the smooth running of the party machine, as they are for party managers today concerned about activists and even ordinary party members going 'off message'.

Michels later described his study as 'a vivisection of the Party, a painful dissection of something living'. Both Weber and Michels (who, unlike Weber, was an active socialist and therefore unable to get a professorial chair in imperial

Germany) were contemptuous of the way the SPD had abandoned its earlier radicalism and concentrated on preserving and developing its own substantial organisational structures. But what for Michels was a cause for despair (the 'cruel game' of the endlessly repeated defeat of democratic hopes) was for Weber just something to be expected.

Michels's analysis puts him among other 'elite theorists' of the late nineteenth and early twentieth centuries, notably Vilfredo Pareto and Gaetano Mosca. Where Marxists focus on class conflict in a process of historical development, elite theorists stress the permanent opposition between elites and masses, with counter-elites periodically replacing the existing ones ('elite circulation') but without changing the basic structure. The term 'elite' suggests the conservative view that elites are in some way better, but elite theory uses it more neutrally and is often critical of old elites and of 'plutocracy', with circulation offering the possibility of renewal. History, said Pareto, is 'the graveyard of aristocracies'. He identified the defenders of the status quo with lions and their cunning challengers with foxes.

The radical US sociologist C. Wright Mills analysed in *The Power Elite* (1956) the interplay between political, economic and military elites.

> In America today there are ... tiers and ranges of wealth and power of which people in the middle and lower ranks know very little ... There are families who ... are quite insulated from the economic jolts and lurches felt by the merely prosperous and those further down the social scale. There are also men of power who in quite small groups make decisions of enormous consequence for the underlying population.

One of these 'men', the Republican president and former general Eisenhower, himself warned in 1961, as he left office, against the 'undue influence' of the 'military-industrial complex'. The British sociologist Ralph Miliband combined elite theory with Marxism in *The State in Capitalist Society* (1969) and was criticised for this by the more orthodox Greek-French Marxist Nicos Poulantzas. The underlying issue was whether the class composition of elites was important, or whether they would behave in the same way wherever they came from – in the vigorous French slogan '*Homme élu, homme foutu*' (Once you're elected, you're useless). Social democratic politics, on which Miliband also wrote, provided some evidence here, as did, more dramatically, the state socialist dictatorships of the twentieth century. Elites certainly 'circulated' in Stalin's Soviet Union, drawn increasingly from the working class, but the upper reaches of the nomenklatura lived a very different life from ordinary Soviet citizens, with special shops, hospitals and so on.

Along with, and linked to, elite theory, theories of 'mass society' were also influential in the early twentieth century. Tocqueville had already expressed anxieties about what he saw as the homogeneity and conformism of North American society. 'The more equal the conditions of men become and the less strong men individually are, the more easily they give way to the current of the multitude and the more difficult it is for them to adhere by themselves to an opinion which the multitude discard.' Durkheim had also been concerned about the normlessness (anomie) of modern societies. In the twentieth century the anonymous and unstructured (and often urban) masses are also seen in two contradictory ways: as inert and passive but also as open to manipulation by demagogic elites and liable to turn into dangerous mobs.

Fascism in the 1920s and 1930s seemed to confirm this diagnosis, with fascists themselves celebrating charismatic leadership (the Nazi *Führerprinzip*) exercised over masses conceived as passive, female and so on. Fascism could in some ways be seen as putting elite theory and mass society theory into practice, embellished with a hopelessly mis-understood version of the Nietzschean superman and the German nationalist conception of the Herrenvolk. The tragi-comic *Lebensborn* breeding programme of the Nazis complemented the pure tragedy of their extermination policies.

Both Sombart and Michels moved from the radical left of politics to positions close to fascism. Sombart's initially sympathetic book on the socialist movement, first published in 1896, had become strongly anti-socialist by the tenth edition in 1924; the last version, in 1934, was called *Deutscher Sozialismus* and supported Nazism. Unlike two other prominent Nazi supporters, the philosopher Martin Heidegger and the legal and political theorist Carl Schmitt, Sombart has not so far been taken up in later social theory, though his economic analysis and his account of the origins of capitalism deserve comparison with Weber's, and his work on war and the state prefigures the turn of social theory in the late twentieth century to pay some belated attention to warfare.

Michels's move towards fascism seems to have been

motivated more by a sense of the impotence of socialism, including revolutionary syndicalism focused on trade unions. Mussolini himself had been a socialist, and his early propaganda portrayed him as a radical, charismatic figure who could cut through red tape and provide political direction. Max Weber had earlier called for a constitution for post-war Germany with a directly elected president for just these reasons, and his analysis also influenced Michels. Like Sombart, Michels eventually became disillusioned with fascism.

Other social theorists, including Marxists and Frankfurt School critical theorists, tried to explain the rise of fascism and Nazism. Of the resources provided by the earlier classical theorists, one was Marx's conception of Bonapartism, with its theme of an authoritarian leader, such as Napoleon I and Marx's contemporary Napoleon III, presiding over a society with relatively unstructured classes. Marx pointed in particular to the French peasantry, which was of course dispersed over the country and therefore unable to act as a class, as he hoped the more urban industrial proletariat would do eventually. He described what has come to be known as Bonapartism as the 'despotism of an individual' where 'all classes were equally powerless'. In fascism, too, class action was banned, trade unions were replaced by corporative structures including employers as well as workers and the regime propagated an ideology of the nation or, in Nazism, the 'people's community' (*Volksgemeinschaft*).

Another approach drew on Weber's more descriptive concept of charismatic leadership, breaking with tradition and with formal or legal-rational forms of rule. Weber's idea of the 'routinisation of charisma', the transformation of the original form of rule into more regulated or traditional channels, is a useful way of thinking about the post-fascist regimes of Franco in Spain and Salazar in Portugal, which survived into the 1970s. The more extreme fascist regimes of Italy and Germany lost the war they provoked and we can only guess how they might otherwise have mutated over time.

Marxists tended to portray fascism as an alternative form of bourgeois class rule. The bourgeois class, fearing the rise of the workers, welcomed the prospect of a non-democratic regime that would keep them in place. But even if you accept the idea that politics is basically about class conflict, this explanation fails to explain how such movements came about and achieved mass support. It's true that capitalists provided funds for fascist leaders, but only when they were relatively well established and had a realistic prospect of power.

Critical theory's openness to cultural issues and Freudian theory arguably allowed it to give a better account of the appeal of fascism than orthodox Marxism. The post-war research project in the US on the 'authoritarian personality', to which Theodor Adorno contributed and which followed the approach of earlier projects in Germany before the war, aimed to identify latently fascist attitudes, measured by the rather obviously named F-scale. An attitude to authority sometimes illustrated by the posture of a cyclist (apologies to cyclist readers!), bent down subserviently to those above and kicking down on those below, seemed to capture important aspects of fascist ideology, with its heroisation of leadership figures and scapegoating of those defined as outsiders. These attitudes could go along with radical criticism of the rich, which was an important feature of early fascist programmes and helped to attract former socialists. (This process can be seen in contemporary politics, where in France, for example, the extreme-right Front National drew support from people who had formerly voted for the Communist Party.)

As we saw in Chapter 5, Norbert Elias, who, with Karl Mannheim, had shared office space in Frankfurt but little else with the early critical theorists, brilliantly traced a parallel between etiquette in early modern Europe and the rise of the modern state, which secured its territorial space at the same time as (some of) its citizens were paying closer attention to their own and others' *personal* space. This 'process of civilisation' also allowed for regressive decivilising processes, and in a book published just before his death in 1990, *The Germans*, Elias analysed these in the authoritarian traditions of Germany in what he described as a 'biography' of a state-society. As he wrote in the Introduction, 'Standing half-hidden in the background . . . is an eyewitness who has lived for nearly ninety years through the events concerned as they unfolded.' Repeating the trajectory of *The Civilizing Process* (1978), Elias begins with a discussion of the persistence of duelling in early twentieth-century imperial Germany before moving on to questions of political structures, nationalism and violence.

By coincidence, the original edition of Elias's book was published in the same year as Zygmunt Bauman's *Modernity and the Holocaust*. Bauman has less to say about the specifically German origins of the Holocaust, focusing instead on the search for order in all modern societies summed up in his 'gardening' image (apologies to gardeners as well as cyclists!). Just as the gardener nurtures plants and aims to eradicate weeds, the Nazis valorised people defined as 'Aryans' and persecuted Jews, Roma, homosexuals and the disabled, as well as their political opponents.

Elias briskly but brilliantly summarises late nineteenth-century German history in the sentence that in 1871 'the victory of the German armies over France was at the same time a victory of the German nobility over the German middle class'. Liberal and democratic ideas were pushed into the background and their apparent triumph in the Weimar Republic was illusory. So Germany was a bit special, but not that special. Playing on the distinction between 'white' and 'black' magic, Elias suggests that Nazism was a throwback, a 'black ideology, full of ideas more appropriate to a pre-industrial world'. He converges, however, with Bauman in the judgement that 'National Socialism revealed . . . tendencies of thinking and acting which can also be found elsewhere'.

Here, then, we see in an extreme example the contribution that social theory can make to the analysis of political and military processes. Nazism was not just militaristic and totalitarian; it also had deep historical and social roots. It is no accident that social theorists like Martin Shaw and Michael Mann have been prominent in genocide studies.

How have social theorists analysed the state? What do we mean by the state? Something more than just governments, administrative bureaucracies, armies and so on, a state is also a legal entity, capable of signing treaties with other states. It is a normative power too, claiming rights of life and death over its citizens and residents, and a base of economic as well as political power. In addition, the modern state has been a main focus and source of political symbolism, since Louis XIV or earlier. Schoolchildren are sometimes taught that Louis was simply vain: in fact he was a smooth and innovative political operator.

The modern concept of the state emerged in Europe around the middle of the last millennium, though in some languages, including English and French, the word can also refer to a condition, as in 'my office is in an untidy state'. What you mostly have in early modern Europe is a mixture of city-states like Venice or Florence, empires like the Ottoman Empire or the Holy Roman Empire, and monarchies like England, Scotland, France or Poland. The independent national state becomes the dominant pattern in Europe by the mid-seventeenth century, often associated with the Peace of Westphalia in 1648, which ended the Thirty Years War in central Europe. These states develop their administrative systems and often engage in what has been called 'internal colonialism', extending state power to peripheral regions, marginalising local languages like Welsh, Gaelic and Breton and, by the nineteenth century, establishing national systems of welfare, education, censuses and so on.

The last partly European land empire, the Ottoman Empire, ceased to exist after the First World War, though many European states retained colonial empires outside Europe for another few decades, leaving a large number of new national states in the late twentieth century. The Soviet Union also retained many of the features of the Russian Empire, especially when it subordinated much of eastern and central Europe from the end of the Second World War until 1989. What is now the European Union, emerging from the 1950s onwards, has some features of an empire (multinational, with multiple citizenships, multilingual, decentralised, etc.). It is, however, democratic, as empires were not. (The member states are required to be democratic, even if the EU's own political arrangements are not, or not very.)

Let's start again with Montesquieu in the mid-eighteenth century. In Chapter 1 we saw how he related the state and other political and legal forms to their roots in broader social processes. He uses the term 'state' much as we do today, both to refer descriptively to one state among others and in a way that differentiates between state and society and within the state between, for example, judicial and executive power. Nearly a century later, Tocqueville deliberately used a term, 'democracy', that covered both political and broader social structures, and his book on America is substantially concerned with the interplay between the two.

With Marx, we have the familiar distinction between base and superstructure and, unfortunately, the fact that he did not live to complete the planned volumes of *Capital* on the state. Engels, as we saw, did write about the state, but otherwise offers only the passing remark that he and Marx had underplayed the importance of political processes in order to stress the overwhelming importance of forms of production. Weber's stress on class, status and party as forms of distribution of *power* reinforced this focus on what Marx called superstructure, and Weber's institutional approach (he was a lawyer before he became a sociologist) stressed the interests of the state apparatus. Bureaucrats have of course a class position and political preferences, but their actions tend to be more directly influenced by internal competition to expand and control their domains of activity. (Remember the civil servant's defence in *Yes, Minister* of the hospital with no patients which ran very smoothly . . .)

Lenin produced an interesting analysis of the state but then forgot it when he inherited the tsarist state and its institutions, including the secret police. As Gramsci wrote from his Fascist prison, 'In the East the State was everything, civil society was primordial and gelatinous; in the West, there was a proper relation between State and civil society, and when the State trembled a sturdy structure of civil society was at once revealed.' Whereas in Russia it had been essential to capture the state, as the Bolsheviks had done in 1917, in the West it was more important to work through civil society and achieve ideological 'hegemony'.

The Marxist state theories of the 1970s and 1980s drew heavily on Gramsci, but there was also a tendency to reduce the capitalist state to a rather undifferentiated expression of capitalism; some West German theorists explicitly referred to the 'derivation' of the state from relations of economic production. It is not difficult to find books on the state from that period which make no reference to any existing state.

The term 'civil society' was also exceptionally prominent in the 1980s, as new social movements in the West and dissidents in the East developed their activity outside state institutions. Non-Marxist sociologists as well as Marxists had tended to prioritise society over the state, but in sociology there was a substantial countercurrent in the 1980s, with Theda Skocpol in the US talking in 1985 about 'bringing the state back in', having focused on state collapse, as well as the movements challenging the state, in an earlier book, *States and Social Revolutions* (1979), on the French, Russian and Chinese revolutions. Weber's emphasis on the state apparatus seemed relevant once more. The 1989 revolutions in communist Europe were a dramatic illustration of this approach. What looked like massively well-defended dictatorships, with huge armies and 'security services', fell apart in the face of a few peaceful demonstrations animated mostly by tiny groups of dissidents.

Tensions between the social and the political appear in the social sciences in the opposition between 'state-centred' and 'society-centred' explanations. To repeat the point, sociologists have tended to prioritise society over the state, while political scientists tend, not surprisingly, to prioritise the state and the political process. A major area of research has been on welfare policies. Why do some countries have better welfare states than others? Why is state-financed health care still controversial in the US? Is it because of the way government is organised, or because of bigger differences in the structure of US capitalism, class structure or values and political culture?

Theories which emphasise the state were challenged in the 1990s when the term 'globalisation' burst on the scene. (I was editing a dictionary of social thought at the beginning of that decade and realised just in time that we needed an entry on this newly fashionable concept.) An extreme version of globalisation theory says that states are becoming or have become irrelevant in the modern world, which is dominated instead by flows of capital, labour and ideas, and other cultural forms. Like the American general who was told at the end of the Second World War that he was flying over Belgium and replied that he didn't want to be bothered by trivial details, extreme globalisers urge that we should drop references to national states from our analysis. Not many globalisation theorists go quite this far, but a common theme is that the national state has been pushed into the background by transnational entities like the European Union or the World Trade Organization, or by international migration. Citizenship used to be a big deal; most countries still have some sort of ceremony for the naturalisation of residents who don't have citizenship by birth or descent. But if you're a diaspora Palestinian you may have a passport from Jordan, Egypt, the UK, the US or wherever; people with multiple passports may choose which one to use as casually as you choose whether to pay a bill with Visa or MasterCard.

Early theories of globalisation tended to stress its economic aspects, but social theorists quickly pointed out its wider social and cultural dimensions. Interestingly, Anthony Giddens and Martin Shaw, two of the British sociologists who had been most prominent in writing in the 1980s about national states and their interrelations, were also in the forefront of globalisation theory. Giddens even 'performed' globalisation in a 1999 lecture series on the topic for the BBC which took place not just in its studios but in front of audiences in London, Hong Kong, Delhi and Washington.[1] His first lecture began with a reference to a friend visiting a remote central African village and finding her hosts viewing and discussing the Hollywood film *Basic Instinct*. Shaw speculated in 2000 about the emergence of a global state anchored in Europe, North America and Japan but operating at a level above even the largest national states and increasingly coordinating their activities. The Transatlantic Trade and Investment Partnership, between the US and Europe, and the Trans-Pacific Partnership, between the US (and some other American countries) and the other side of the Pacific, which may both be in force by the time this book is published, are current examples.

Once again, we can see how important it is to approach a topic as vast as globalisation with a framework that doesn't isolate its economic, political and cultural aspects but studies their interrelations. McDonald's is a cultural as well as an economic phenomenon, and also biological, as seen in the disastrous impact recently of 'Western' fast food on the health of populations in Asia and Africa. Political movements are increasingly global as well: 'Jihad vs. McWorld' may be a simplification, but it captures an important aspect of globalisation and diaspora politics.

Finally, we might ask whether politics is changing in Western democracies. The relative immobility of political structures (parliaments, elections, parties, etc.) contrasts strikingly with the dramatic advances in means of communication and what in Russia has come to be called 'political technology'. Theories of 'post-democracy' suggest that behind the continuing forms of democratic politics its substance has been eroded by techniques of mass manipulation by control of television and other media and the rise of populist parties, such as Berlusconi's Forza Italia, which ruled briefly in the mid-1990s and again from 2001 to 2006. (See David Runciman's *Politics* in this series for a fuller analysis.)

8

UNFINISHED BUSINESS

This book aims to bring out the richness and relevance of social theory. There are, however, areas that its practitioners have been slow to address. First, despite the major contributions discussed in the previous chapter, international relations and warfare were barely present in sociology throughout Europe's second 'thirty years war', from 1914 to 1945, and the cold war that immediately followed it. If you take a look at titles of sociology books and articles in the mid- to late twentieth century containing the word 'conflict' you'll find lots on industrial conflict and (especially in the 1970s) quite a lot on class conflict and (again from the 1970s onwards) on gender conflicts, but remarkably few on international conflict and warfare.

Part of the explanation may be 'methodological nationalism', in which 'society' was understood in terms of the nation-state (British society, French society, etc.). Although Raymond Aron in France and to some extent C. Wright Mills in the US did address issues of war and peace, it was not until the 1980s that Anthony Giddens, Martin Shaw and Michael Mann put them at the centre of attention. (Both Aron and Wright Mills were somewhat marginalised in France and the US respectively, Aron for his anti-Marxist liberalism and Wright Mills for his leftism.) The emergent academic subject of international relations had its main background in diplomatic history, with only a minority seeing it as a sociology of the international.

Then there is the whole issue of European colonialism and racism, including that of North America. Sociologists were slow to move into post-colonial theory, which remains stronger in literary studies than in the social sciences, and more prominent in the UK, America and Australasia than in much of continental Europe. Questions of race were to some extent put on the social theory agenda by the US Civil Rights movement of the 1960s and gender by the feminist movements a little later, but social theorists remained predominantly white and male. Social science tended to avoid using the term 'race', seen as irrevocably contaminated by European racism, and blurred the issue in a blander concept of 'ethnicity'.

The challenge of post-colonial theory to social theory is, I think, fourfold. First, the history of European philosophy and the emergent social sciences needs to be rethought. The Australian theorist Raewyn Connell has pointed out that early sociology did write very substantially about non-European societies, but usually in a way that emphasised the 'difference between the civilisation of the metropole and other cultures whose main feature was their primitiveness . . . Sociology was formed within the culture of imperialism, and embodied an intellectual response to the colonised world.' Second, theories of modernity need to take account of the interplay between Europe (in an extended sense that includes at least North America) and the rest of the world. Third, the colonial past of much of the world, whether as coloniser or colonised, deserves more attention than it has received. Finally, we should note the intersection of theories of race, notably work by African-Americans, and post-colonial theory and critical race theory in North America and Europe. Once again, recent developments in social theory have revived interest in earlier work. Post-colonial theory in the US has led to renewed attention, for example, to the work of the African-American sociologist and activist W. E. B. Du Bois.

The relation between the social and the biological was also neglected because of false starts in the past, in what Weber attacked as 'zoological' racism and which reached its absurd and lethal culmination in Nazi 'racial science'. Rejecting 'socio-biology' and its crude notions of evolutionary competition applied to the social world of humans as well as other animals, sociologists steered clear of the whole issue of the rooting of social processes in biological ones and of societies in their natural environments. The 'green' movements of the same period did not have much impact on social theory, apart from Ulrich Beck's idea of 'risk society', and the depth of the global environmental crisis is only now coming to be recognised. In 2013, Beck began a major European Research Council project on climate change.[1]

All these remain challenges for social theory to address later in this century. The biggest challenge of all is perhaps to the very idea of social theory: the question of whether we are heading not just to a post-democratic but to a 'post-social' world of increasing individualisation and a decreasing sense that social problems are amenable to social (and political) solutions. One way of posing these issues that was particularly prominent in the later twentieth century was in theories of 'postmodernity'. As we saw in Chapter 5, post-modern theory spans literary, cultural and social theory, with offshoots even in theories of postmodern war or post-modern accounting. The underlying idea is, however, that of fragmentation, whether of historical narratives, employment relations, aesthetic styles or family structures.

Take work as an example. There used to be a notion in industrial societies that a typical work life involved working for a single employer for something like forty hours a week, forty-plus weeks of the year for forty years, followed by retirement and death. 'Fordist' production, whether or not it was based on assembly lines, involved massive factories and production units oriented to a mass market. Along with this stereotype was a family model of monogamous marriage with two or three children lasting, with luck, a similar forty years or so. Accounts of history, whether liberal or Marxist, also tended to be shaped in terms of an evolutionary narrative of progress. What in Britain was called Whig history (the name taken from the early Liberal Party) was mocked for beginning with the Flood and running through in a linear way to the reign of George III. Engels wrote speculatively about 'the part played by labour in the transition from ape to man', and in the more recent past the US thinker Francis Fukuyama announced in 1989, just before the anti-communist revolutions in Europe, the 'end of history' marked by the unchallenged hegemony of liberal capitalist democracy.

These images of modernity were accompanied in sociology by a strong conception of society, which we have seen most clearly with Durkheim. Society gives us our identity, our morality, our religion and so on. Modern politics became a politics of mass electorates and mass parties (beginning with the socialists and then with the bourgeois parties catching up). State administration was similarly massive and bureaucratic, with surveillance extended over the national territory in statistics, censuses and regulations. (It was said of the French Third Republic in the late nineteenth and early twentieth centuries that the minister of education could know that at a given time, say 10 a.m. on a Tuesday in October, all pupils across the country would be doing the same lesson.) Political ideologies, too, tended to be formalised, with massive tracts and speeches. Communism, coming late on the scene in the early twentieth century in Russia and mid-century in eastern and central Europe and east and south-east Asia, took this to an extreme, with central planning of economies and an ideology of 'scientific communism' that was a compulsory part of higher education curricula.

Postmodern theory questioned all formal systems, whether of history ('grand narratives') or of society. In a related move, the French current of ideas known (mostly outside France) as 'post-structuralism' questioned the binary oppositions governing structuralist approaches in linguistics, social anthropology and other areas of the human sciences. Everything was much more fragmented and jumbled than structuralists or modernists believed, and we had to live with this uncertainty. The stark simplicity of modernist architecture was replaced by playful and decorative elements taken at random from past ages.

I have presented this opposition between modernity

and postmodernity in simplistic terms, but even the most sophisticated expressions of the contrast were simplistic in their description of modernism. The architectural image can't easily be extended to literature, where modernists were much more sceptical and tentative in what they wrote. In social theory, while Durkheim often sounds, and was, dogmatic, and he did write _The_ Rules of Sociological Method, his contemporary Weber qualifies almost every assertion he makes – often in the same sentence. Bauman flirted for a time with the language of postmodernity, but then settled on his rather more cautious image of 'liquid' modernity and its various expressions in work, love, culture and so on.

As I suggested in Chapter 5, there is clearly something real about our current social situation that is captured in theories of postmodernity or liquid modernity. However, others, including myself, have preferred to talk about a shift from earlier, confident forms of modernity to a more cautious or, as Giddens called it, 'reflexive' phase – what Ulrich Beck called second modernity. Who can now write confidently about 'progress' without worrying about Eurocentrism or climate change? Anti-democratic challenges have become increasingly explicit. In social theory, there has been a shift from formal theories such as those of Talcott Parsons or, for that matter, Marxists also attracted by system theory to more informal approaches, such as Giddens's 'structuration theory', which offers a set of concepts and pointers to relevant aspects of social reality rather than aiming to formulate testable propositions.

In the course of this book I have been suggesting that we need a rather broad understanding of what we mean by a theory anyway. At its most basic, the term suggests any framework which describes or explains something. I can say I have a 'theory' about where the mouse in my kitchen has its nest. What makes this more than just a guess, prediction or hypothesis is that I may be able to back it up with some generalisations about hiding places, food sources and so on; an animal biologist with the right specialism, or for that matter an exterminator, would have a much larger body of background knowledge.

Some theories can be summarised in algebra, like $E = mc^2$ in physics, or other formulae, often much longer, in economics or parts of the other social sciences. (I once watched Jacques Delors, when he was economics minister and interviewed on French TV, drawing on a flip chart to illustrate a point – something that would have ended the political career of a British or US treasury minister.) Alternatively, the symbols may just be used to describe a process, as when Marx contrasted the exchange of one commodity for another via money (C-M-C) with the purchase and sale of commodities for the sake of monetary gain (M-C-M^1), where the second M is greater than the first, or if I summarise his distinction between base and superstructure by writing the latter over the former:

$$\frac{\text{superstructure}}{\text{base}}$$

Here a suspicious reader may think I'm just using the diagram to make the claim look more scientific.

Something like this suspicion may be behind the

tendency for social theorists to make less use of formal dia-
grams and models than in the past. The very idea of formal
theory is probably in decline. We have, in other words,
become less like Marx and more like Weber, offering a set
of categories to describe social reality and a set of processes,
like Weber's 'rationalisation', to look out for when formulat-
ing our descriptions. This is perhaps because most of the
time we are asking how and why something we know to
exist has come to exist in the way it does. Remember Simmel's reformulation of Kant's question about how (a pure
science of) nature is possible when he asked how society
is possible. Rousseau asked the same question about inequality and political domination; Montesquieu about the
various legal and political regimes he observed around the
world, Marx and Weber about the emergence of capitalism, Durkheim about the division of labour, religion and
the regular variations in suicide rates. Other theorists ask a
similar question about theories. Althusser, for example, can
be read as asking how Marxism, as he understood it, was
possible: what were the philosophical principles underlying
Marx's revolutionary 'science'?

The realist philosophy of science developed by Mary
Hesse, Rom Harré and Roy Bhaskar offers what I consider
to be the most useful way of thinking about scientific
theories. Hesse and Harré stressed the role of theoretical
models, which are always only a partial fit but which,
if successful, capture the essential elements of causal
processes in reality, pointing to tendencies which may or
may not produce observable effects. The tendency of the
polar ice caps to melt as a result of humanly produced

climate change may be temporarily counteracted by other causal processes. Roy Bhaskar asked the following question: given that we have science, what has to be the case for it to be possible? Empiricist philosophers say (rightly) that we have to have experiences of the world. Rationalists like Kant add (rightly) that we also need structuring categories and theories. Bhaskar pointed out that there also needs to be an independently existing world which we attempt to describe and explain with our theories. In open systems we may not be able to predict, but we can explain, with reference to the interaction of structures and mechanisms at different levels of reality (physical, chemical, biological, social, etc.). Bhaskar developed a transformational model of social action which parallels Giddens's structuration theory in spanning individual actions, such as the physical process of writing a cheque, and the structures that make them possible.

Much of natural science, too, is asking why and how things are possible, starting with the existence of the universe itself and the big bang. We are sure about the former and pretty sure about the latter; pragmatist and realist philosophies of social science rightly stress this aspect of science. Why has the pond frozen? It must have been cold last night. Why did the plane crash? Was it a mechanical failure or was it shot down? The difference, perhaps, in the social sciences is that we can ask a further set of 'why?' questions. Suppose my cow dies. The vet may be able to tell me how and why. But suppose I want to know why *my* cow died and not yours, or why it had to be *my* relative who was on the crashed plane? This is where we may turn to ideas of fate, religion and so on. God or fate determined which cow or plane was doomed.

In the social world, and without turning to religion or metaphysics, we can often answer questions of this kind. If the plane *was* shot down, we can ask why, and not just how. If I ask why there is a big river running through what we now call London, a geologist can give me an answer in terms of the movements of glaciers, soil and so on. But a historian can tell me that estuaries are often settled and show how this happened in the case of London, perhaps including some reference to the intentions and purposes of those early Londoners of whom records survive. Here theories of different kinds and explanations at different levels can be combined according to our preferences for explanations of a particular sort or to the direction of our interests. As sea levels rise due to human stupidity, we may come to feel that our ancestors chose what has turned out to be a bad place to live and to found what came to be the capital of England and later of the UK.

We can still wonder how much to make of this difference between the natural and the social world. Durkheim is again a useful reference point. In *Suicide* we can see him discouraging a focus on motives and intentions, though both his early use of the common or collective consciousness and his late book on religion demonstrate the importance he attached to what he called collective ideas or 'representations'. Durkheim's nephew Marcel Mauss suggested in an article of 1927 that there are basically just two things in societies: the group itself, usually on a specific territory, and 'the representations and movements of this group'. This way of putting it leaves open the question whether we should concentrate on the movements or the representations. I think it's pretty clear that Mauss felt they go together. In his book-length classic essay on *The Gift* (1925) he shows how you have to observe both the exchange and the ideas of obligation attached to it by the gift-givers. And in the study of systems of classification that he wrote with Durkheim they show how belief systems such as images of the heavens may map on to spatial divisions in the tribal settlement.

What Durkheim and Mauss share is a strong concept of society: Mauss wrote provocatively in his 1927 essay that there are not social sciences in the plural but 'a science of societies'. Sociologists, as we have seen, disagree over the usefulness of the concept of society. Durkheim uses the term all the time; Weber, in his massive posthumous work *Economy and Society*, uses it just twice – first in scare quotes and then in relation to the concept of a society of estates. He once wrote that he had become a sociologist in order to put an end to the use of collective concepts. In his approach, a sociological conception of, say, the state, as opposed to a legal one, has to be understood as referring to a probability that people will orient their behaviour to their idea of the state, by obeying laws, paying taxes and so on. Collective concepts, he believed, are sociologically wrong and politically dangerous. His anxiety about society did not, however, stretch to another collective concept, culture, which he used quite substantially.

Few people would now defend a strong Durkheimian conception of society, but it is another matter to drop the concept altogether, as Mrs Thatcher did in a throwaway remark, to reduce it to purely economic or political processes, or to reduce even these to something which can be sorted out by a 'technological fix'. Can we solve the problem of global hunger by GM food, of carbon-induced climate change by nuclear fusion, or of war by having robots and drones fighting in our place? What, the sociologist asks, about the social context in which such devices are used?

One influential strand of contemporary social theory, commonly known as 'actor-network theory', suggests that we should drop, or at least bracket out, the natural/social divide and include natural and created objects in our list of actors. As Bruno Latour once said, 'nature' and 'society' are 'cheap' ways of analysing the connections between things that overlook their singularity. In an early study in 1986, Michel Callon suggested that a sociological analysis of the scallop industry in a Breton fishing port had to include as actors not just the fishermen and the experts who were advising them but the scallops themselves. When they cease to behave as predicted he describes them as 'dissidents', with whom the researchers have to conduct 'their longest and most difficult negotiations'. In another study, Latour personalises (and feminises) a rapid-transit vehicle system called Aramis.

Whatever you think of this provocative language, actor-network theory has the advantage of offering an intermediate position between two simplistic conceptions of technology: one that sees it as neutral and shaped only by the purposes of the humans (and maybe some other animals) who use it, and the other, known as technological determinism, that sees us as constrained by our technologies. It also responds to the challenges posed by advances in artificial intelligence, which mean that we may often not be sure if we are interacting with another human or with a machine. We are increasingly reading about the 'post-human' as well as the post-social.

And yet we cannot avoid thinking in social terms even about our relations with (other parts of) nature, just as we tend to object if we are treated 'like machines'. The idea that in order to command nature we have to obey it goes back at least to Francis Bacon and the 'scientific revolution' of the seventeenth century. Some of Bacon's contemporaries thought of animals as machines, but others were moving towards a more modern view. This is also the time when people began to think about society in the abstract way that seems natural to us (even if, like Thatcher, we reject it); before, it means something much vaguer, like association or companionship.

As I suggested in Chapters 4 and 5, the concept of society remains problematic. If what we now call 'society' has a beginning maybe it also has an end. We seem in many ways to have become more individualistic. Take an equally prom-inent sociological concept like class. On the old model, industrial forms of production cause people to cluster in large occupational communities with similar conditions of life and similar political preferences. Now the large indus-tries have declined, been mechanised or gone global; the occupational structure of a former mining or shipbuild-ing town will be as diverse as anywhere else. People whose grandparents may have voted all their lives for the same party may now vote differently every time. Class influences on life chances intersect with those of ethnicity and gender, geography and household size. New acronyms are coined to describe these differences, such as DINKY, which emerged in the 1980s: Dual Income No Kids (Yet). We now also have the more jokey SITCOM (Single Income Two Children Oppressive Mortgage). Self-employment and contract work have become more common.

This does not mean that class has become irrelevant: class factors still determine individual life chances, but in more diverse and complicated ways. This also affects the influence of class and other structural factors on politics. In our political choices, we are less likely, in J. F. Kennedy's formulation, to ask what we can do for America and more likely to ask what the American (or British, or Scottish) state can do for us. At election time pop-up parties are becoming more common; the old ones tend to stick around but often look a bit dinosaurish or fragile. The French socialist party, for example, nearly disappeared in the early 1990s before bouncing back; by the time this book is published there may not be much left of the British Liberal Democrats, junior partners in government in 2010–15.

In Chapter 5 I mentioned Jean Baudrillard and his announcement of the 'end of the social'. Gilles Lipovetsky wrote similarly of a 'second individualist revolution': postmodernity means 'the predominance of the individual over the universal, of psychology over ideology, of communication over politicization, of diversity over homogeneity, of the permissive over the coercive'. Ulrich Beck, who spoke of a 'second modernity' rather than postmodernity, also stressed the theme of individualisation of class positions and other aspects of social life. Beck differentiates clearly between individualisation and individualism: the first refers to an institutional (or more precisely de-institutionalising) process in modern societies, while individual*ism* refers to a personal attitude. Individualisation may make people *more* dependent on institutions such as mass media and may encourage conformist behaviour.

Durkheim's stress on social facts composed of, but not reducible to, individual behaviour was opposed at the time by Gabriel Tarde, who stressed imitation as the crucial social process producing the same collective effects. Tarde, who had been largely forgotten, was taken up again in post-modern thought and by Bruno Latour as a forerunner of his 'actor-network theory'. If you see an oncoming car with its windscreen wipers going, you may prepare to put on your own even before you hit the rain. Imitation may be conscious or unconscious, which is possibly one of the reasons it appeals to Latour.

But where Latour believes he has gone beyond these oppositions between action and structure or society and the individual, I take the more boring view that we are stuck with them. Sitting at home on my own, I break off to have lunch. I believe myself to be free in this choice, yet it is structured in all sorts of ways. Time and space, for example. I feel uneasy lunching before midday, just as I feel uneasy starting to drink before six. I automatically sit at a table, although no one would know if I ate at my desk, as I sometimes do in my office, or in an armchair. And no one would know if I had bread and jam for lunch, or cake, though in practice I know I will choose something more conventional from the fridge.

Bourdieu and his associates could have explained what I eat in terms of my resources of economic and cultural capital, such as the choice of the healthy apple or orange over the more filling banana. You will already be bored by this trivial example, but at the aggregate level nutritionists and the food industry search for data of this kind.

As I have stressed throughout this short book, the kinds of descriptions and explanations we want are diverse and complementary. An event such as the outbreak of a war can be explained both by a detailed description of political and military decision-making and by larger structural features such as economic or geopolitical competition. We don't need to choose between them, though we may decide for practical reasons to focus on one level and let others deal with the rest.

If Latour were looking over my shoulder he would pounce on my use of the word 'level'. His critique of simplistic ways of conceiving this is well taken, but it remains the case that reality is stratified, even if the strata are jumbled up as in a marble cake rather than in straight lines. Even Marx and Engels, when they wrote in simplified terms about base and superstructure, acknowledged the complicated interplay between them, and this comes to the fore in Marx's analyses of the interplay of economic and political divisions and conflicts in France.

Marx wrote about contemporary themes partly for the sake of the money paid by newspapers, but he was also contributing to what Karl Mannheim later called the 'diagnosis of the times'. This term has recently come back into prominence in the work of Axel Honneth, who has also revived the notion of social pathology, which for a long time was associated with Durkheim's rather problematic attempt to distinguish between the normal and the pathological in human societies. This idea of diagnosis is linked to the growing closeness of social theory and social, moral and political philosophy.

The debates around modernity and postmodernity are one of the key sites of the idea that social theory can and should offer a necessarily tentative attempt at diagnosis of the times. Even if postmodern theory is a bit out of fashion, it continues, like Marxism, to shape a lot of more recent thinking – for example, in theories of 'post-democracy' by Colin Crouch and others. Here, as in earlier 'posts', the emphasis is on the way in which democracy has been not so much replaced by something else (fingers crossed) as undermined from the inside and transformed into more of a façade or theatre, with the real politics taking place else-where, monopolised by those who control finance and the media (the latter, for example, in Italy, where Silvio Ber-lusconi's political power relied heavily on control of the media).

A long-standing and rather dangerous theme of Western social theory has been the idea that, in Engels's phrase, humanity only sets itself problems it can solve. Marx, too, suggested that 'the developed world only shows to the less developed the image of its own future'. A century later, in 1960, the US political economist Walt Rostow wrote of a 'take-off' into a stable society of industrialism and mass consumption, with communism not as the end point of the sequence but a 'disease of the transition' that could affect societies like a burst tyre as your plane takes off. (Once you're at cruising height or, in Rostow's phrase, have moved from the take-off phase into industrialism and 'high mass consumption', things are unlikely to go wrong.) We now know enough about the environmental consequences of industrialisation and mass consumption to realise we may be heading for a hard landing and that urgent social and political questions are as important as ever, if not more so. Just as we can't do without politics, we can't do without social theory.

In Chapter 3 I referred to the evolutionary idea of differentiation. Evolution, whether you see it in naturalistic terms or as a learning process, means differentiation. In school, you study several subjects. If you go on to university, there will probably be fewer, and if you continue to the end of the road and write a PhD it will be even more specialised; a broad title like the title of this book would not be acceptable for a doctoral thesis.

One area where this can clearly be seen is in the sciences themselves, including the social sciences. People don't any longer describe themselves as 'natural philosophers'. In social science, too, most universities will have departments of geography, politics (with or without international relations), sociology (with or without anthropology, media studies or social policy) and so on. Some include sub-disciplines; others have umbrella faculties of 'social studies' or sexier names like 'global studies'. Everyone talks about interdisciplinarity, yet the 'disciplines' remain as organising structures, and even interdisciplinary fields like science studies, climate studies or gender studies develop their own specialisms. We may not have 'paradigms' in Kuhn's strong sense of hegemonic and largely unquestioned 'disciplinary matrices', but we do have organising frameworks or quasi-paradigms which are important social as well as intellectual institutions.

Academic social theory can go in two directions. One is to establish itself as a kind of sub-discipline, distinct from the main fields of philosophy, sociology, politics and so on. An editor taking this view would be happy with what I wrote in the earlier chapters on Rousseau or Durkheim but would chop out the later paragraphs on inequality or suicide studies today. The other approach, which I prefer, is a broader one, spanning the social sciences and the binary divide between social science and 'humanities' and including the social thought generated by social movements and others outside the academy.

You might call this approach promiscuous; I prefer to call it cosmopolitan. Cosmopolitanism is risky: feeling sort of at home in lots of places or languages may leave you feeling not quite at home anywhere. The greater danger is that the bureaucratic mind likes identities to be clear-cut: ideally people should have just one passport and be born in the country whose name is on the cover. (You might expect an immigrant nation like the US to be an exception, but even there you have to be American-born to become president, as we were reminded by the ridiculous fuss when Obama was elected.) A cosmopolitan frame of reference also has other risks, as we saw in relation to inequality. If I worry about inequality in my own country, should I really be worrying more about inequalities across Europe or worldwide?

Academic disciplines are in many ways like countries. They come and go, but mostly they remain. However, the burden of proof is on those who maintain borders to justify them. Social theory offers a border-free space and a passport to move between or to settle in more bordered spaces. Sociology, which has been my disciplinary home throughout my career, has a special place here. Since its invention in the late nineteenth century, it has always been open to other, slightly older disciplines, and it has itself displayed a kind of soft imperialism. Political science studies politics, economics studies economic processes, but what do sociology and social anthropology study? If we say social processes, we immediately have to say that political and economic processes are also social.

In sociology, 'theory' remains a core element though somewhat in decline, at least in the English-speaking countries, and social theory programmes often lead a precarious existence. In the wider scene of publishing and the public sphere, however, theorists like Judith Butler, Jürgen Habermas and Slavoj Žižek enjoy celebrity status. The wave of social theory that broke in the 1970s continues to irrigate (and sometimes irritate) the social sciences and philosophy, as well as spreading more broadly. This book aims to widen the spread.

FURTHER INVESTIGATIONS

INTRODUCTION

As general background, see, for example, William Outhwaite, 'Theory', in Martin Holborn (ed.), *Contemporary Sociology* (Cambridge, Polity Press, 2015), or Ralph Fevre and Angus Bancroft, *Dead White Men and Other Important People: Sociology's Big Ideas* (Basingstoke, Palgrave Macmillan, 2010). For more detailed accounts, see Larry J. Ray, *Theorizing Classical Sociology* (Buckingham, Open University Press, 1999) and Austin Harrington (ed.), *Modern Social Theory* (Oxford, Oxford University Press, 2005).

There are also a lot of good edited collections of original texts. I strongly recommend these, as there's nothing like reading the classical theorists themselves. I've included some below, but see also, for instance, Craig Calhoun et al. (eds), *Classical Sociological Theory and Contemporary Sociological Theory* (Oxford, Wiley-Blackwell, 2012).

1 ORIGINS

See Johan Heilbron, *The Rise of Social Theory* (Cambridge, Polity Press, 1995), and Brian Singer, *Montesquieu and the Discovery of the Social* (Basingstoke, Palgrave Macmillan, 2013). Still worth reading is Durkheim's *Montesquieu and*

Rousseau: Forerunners of Sociology (Ann Arbor, University of Michigan Press, 1960).

On inequality, see Richard Wilkinson and Kate Pickett, *The Spirit Level: Why Equality is Better for Everyone* (London, Allen Lane, 2009), Daniel Dorling, *Injustice: Why Social Inequality Persists* (Bristol, Policy Press, 2011), and Thomas Piketty, *Capital in the Twenty-First Century* (Cambridge, MA, Belknap Press, 2014).

2 CAPITALISM

The work of Marx and Marxists is substantially available online: see https://www.marxists.org/archive/marx/.

Of short published selections in English, one of the first and still the best is Tom Bottomore and Maximilien Rubel (eds), *Karl Marx: Writings on Sociology and Social Philosophy* (Harmondsworth, Penguin, 1967).

For a critical discussion of social theories of capitalism, see Tom Bottomore, *Theories of Modern Capitalism* (London, George Allen & Unwin, 1985).

For a contemporary critique of capitalism, see, for example, David Harvey, *Seventeen Contradictions and the End of Capitalism* (London, Profile, 2014), and also Colin Crouch, *Making Capitalism Fit for Society* (Cambridge, Polity Press, 2013).

3 SOCIETY

Durkheim has to be the main focus here. My book *The Future of Society* (Oxford, Wiley-Blackwell, 2006) traces earlier and later analyses. A good selection in English of Durkheim's work is Kenneth Thompson (ed.), *Readings from Emile Durkheim* (London, Taylor and Francis, 2004).

Secondary works on Durkheim include Gianfranco Poggi, *Durkheim* (Oxford, Oxford University Press, 2000), and the more comprehensive books by Steven Lukes, *Emile Durkheim: His Life and Work* (Harmondsworth, Penguin, 1973; Stanford, Stanford University Press, 1985), and, more recently, Marcel Fournier, *Emile Durkheim: A Biography* (Cambridge, Polity Press, 2012).

4 ORIGINS OF CAPITALISM AND THEORIES OF SOCIAL ACTION

When Max Weber wrote about the origins of capitalism, he was also developing the analysis of social action, which he presented most systematically in his posthumously published book *Economy and Society* (Berkeley, University of California Press, 1978). Much shorter and more readable is Max Weber, *The Protestant Ethic and the Spirit of Capitalism*. Of the various editions, the best translation is Stephen Kalberg's (New York, Oxford University Press, 2010).

The best translated selection of Weber's work is in W. G. Runciman (ed.), *Max Weber: Selections in Translation*, translated by Eric Matthews (Cambridge, Cambridge

University Press, 1978). The massive secondary literature includes, notably, the systematic overview of his work in Martin Albrow, *Max Weber's Construction of Social Theory* (Basingstoke, Macmillan Education, 1990) .

The most recent and comprehensive biography of Weber, whose first biography was written by his wife, the feminist theorist Marianne Weber, is by Joachim Radkau, *Max Weber: A Biography*, translated by Patrick Camiller (Cambridge, Polity Press, 2009).

For an early classic comparison of Weber and Marx see the 1932 essay by Karl Löwith, *Max Weber and Karl Marx*, edited by Tom Bottomore and William Outhwaite, with a preface to the new edition by Bryan S. Turner (London, Routledge, 1993).

See also Martin Hollis and Steve Smith, *Understanding and Explaining International Relations* (Oxford, Oxford University Press, 1991). Although its focus is on international relations, the book brilliantly and economically presents the alternatives between individualistic and more holistic and structural approaches to social theory and between an emphasis on causal explanation or interpretive understanding.

5 HOW IS SOCIETY POSSIBLE?

Works by and on Simmel are available online: see http://www.socio.ch/sim/index_sim.htm.

David Frisby, *Sociological Impressionism: A Reassessment of Georg Simmel's Social Theory* (London, Routledge,

1992), remains probably the best guide to Simmel's work. On 'phenomenological' sociology, see Steven Vaitkus, 'Phenomenology and Sociology', in Bryan S. Turner (ed.), *The Blackwell Companion to Social Theory* (Oxford, Blackwell, 2nd edn, 2000).

An explicit theory of what came to be called social constructionism is given in Peter Berger and Thomas Luckmann, *The Social Construction of Reality* (1966; Harmondsworth, Penguin, 1967).

See also Harold Garfinkel, *Studies in Ethnomethodology* (1967; New York, Wiley, 1991).

6 DISCOVERING THE UNCONSCIOUS

Freud's writings are substantially available online: see http://wikilivres.ca/wiki/Sigmund_Freud.

For an excellent discussion of the relationship between psychoanalysis and social theories of modernity, see Harvey Ferguson, *The Lure of Dreams: Sigmund Freud and the Construction of Modernity* (London, Routledge, 1996). See also Laura Marcus, *Dreams of Modernity: Psychoanalysis, Literature, Cinema* (New York, Cambridge University Press, 2014).

For shorter introductions to Freud, see Richard Wollheim, *Freud* (London, Fontana, 2nd edn, 1991) or, for a more basic introduction, Pamela Thurschwell, *Sigmund Freud* (London, Routledge, 2000). Peter Gay, *Freud for Historians* (New York, Oxford University Press, 1985), is also relevant more broadly to the humanities and social sciences.

7 SOCIAL THEORY AND POLITICS

Two classical contributions are those by Werner Sombart, *Why is There No Socialism in the United States?* (London, Macmillan, 1976), and Robert Michels, *Political Parties* (New York, Free Press, 1962).

David Beetham, 'Liberal Democracy and the Limits of Democratization', in David Held (ed.), *Prospects for Democracy* (Cambridge, Polity Press, 1993), focuses on Michels and related issues.

Bob Jessop, *State Power* (Cambridge, Polity Press, 2008), presents his developed analysis of the state and is the best guide to it.

8 UNFINISHED BUSINESS

On the relation between 'European' modernity and the rest of the world, see Peter Wagner, *Modernity: Understanding the Present* (Cambridge, Polity Press, 2012). On the implications of post-colonial theory for social theory, see Gurminder K. Bhambra, *Rethinking Modernity: Postcolonialism and the Modern Imagination* (Basingstoke, Palgrave Macmillan, 2007), and *Connected Sociologies* (London, Bloomsbury, 2014). See also Raewyn Connell, *Southern Theory: The Global Dynamics of Knowledge in Social Science* (Sydney, Allen and Unwin, 2007). For a particularly insightful and readable critical take on sociology, see Charles Turner, *Investigating Sociological Theory* (London, Sage, 2010).

In addition to the websites mentioned earlier, there are good sites on the work of more recent theorists, notably:

Bourdieu
hyperbourdieu.jku.at/hyperbourdieustart.html

Elias
www.norberteliasfoundation.nl/

Foucault
michel-foucault-archives.org/?-Online-Archives-&lang=en

and *Habermas*
www.habermasforum.dk/

NOTES

CHAPTER 1

1. See, for example, http://www.bbc.co.uk/news/business-16545898
2. http://www.oecd-ilibrary.org/social-issues-migration-health/trends-in-income-inequality-and-its-impact-on-economic-growth_5jxrjncwxv6j-en

CHAPTER 7

1. http://www.bbc.co.uk/radio4/reith1999/

CHAPTER 8

1. http://erc.europa.eu/methodological-cosmopolitan-ism-laboratory-climate-change

INDEX

IDEAS IN PROFILE
SMALL INTRODUCTIONS TO BIG TOPICS

Ideas in Profile is a landmark series that offers concise and entertaining introductions to topics that matter.

ALREADY PUBLISHED

Politics
by David Runciman

Art in History
by Martin Kemp

Shakespeare
by Paul Edmondson

The Ancient World
by Jerry Toner

FORTHCOMING

Geography
by Carl Lee and
Danny Dorling

Criticism
by Catherine Belsey

Music
by Andrew Gant

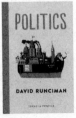

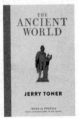